Troilus and Cressida, All's Well That Ends Well, and *Measure for Measure*

An Annotated Bibliography of Shakespeare Studies
1662–2004

PEGASUS SHAKESPEARE BIBLIOGRAPHIES

General Editor
RICHARD L. NOCHIMSON
Yeshiva University

Troilus and Cressida, All's Well That Ends Well,
and *Measure for Measure*

An Annotated Bibliography of Shakespeare Studies
1662–2004

Edited by
BARBARA HOWARD TRAISTER

Pegasus Press
ASHEVILLE, NC, AND CHANDLER, AZ
2005

© Copyright 2005
Pegasus Press
ASHEVILLE, NC, AND CHANDLER, AZ

www.pegpress.org

Library of Congress Cataloguing-in-Publication Data
Traister, Barbara Howard.
    Troilus and Cressida, All's well that ends well, and Measure for measure : an annotated bibliography of Shakespeare studies, 1662–2004 / edited by Barbara Howard Traister.
    p. cm. — (Pegasus Shakespeare bibliographies)
Includes bibliographical references and indexes.
ISBN 1-889818-44-5 (alk. paper)
    1. Shakespeare, William, 1564–1616. Troilus and Cressida — Bibliography. 2. Shakespeare, William, 1564–1616. Measure for measure — Bibliography. 3. Shakespeare, William, 1564–1616. As you like it — Bibliography. 4. Troilus (legendary character) in literature — Bibliography. 5. Trojan War — Literature and the war — Bibliography. 6. Troy (Extinct city) — In literature — Bibliography. 7. Cressida (Fictitious character) — Bibliography. I. Title. II. Series.
Z8812.T7T73 2005
[PR2836]
822.3'3—dc22   2005048900

Cover: The trimming of Thomas Nashe Gentleman, by the high-tituled patron Don Richardo de Medico campo, barber chirurgion to Trinitie Colledge in Cambridge (London, 1597). By permission of the Van Pelt-Dietrich Library, University of Pennsylvania.

This book has been typeset in Garamond
at Pegasus Press and has been made to last.
It is printed on acid-free paper
to library specifications.

Printed in the United States of America.

CONTENTS

Preface	vii
List of Abbreviations	xi

I. Editions of Shakespeare's Plays and Basic Reference Works
  A. Single-Volume Editions of Shakespeare's Plays ... 1
  B. Multi-Volume Editions of Shakespeare's Plays ... 4
  C. Basic Reference Works for Shakespeare Studies ... 8

II. Problem Plays as a Group ... 18

III. *Troilus and Cressida*
  A. Editions ... 26
  B. Dating and Textual Studies ... 29
  C. Influences; Sources; Historical and Intellectual Backgrounds; Topicality ... 31
  D. Language and Linguistics ... 35
  E. Criticism ... 37
  F. Stage History; Productions; Performance Criticism; Film and Television Versions ... 49
  G. Adaptations; Play as Source for and Influence on Later Writers and Works ... 54
  H. Bibliographies ... 54

IV. *All's Well That Ends Well*
  A. Editions ... 55
  B. Dating and Textual Studies ... 56
  C. Influences; Sources; Historical and Intellectual Backgrounds; Topicality ... 58
  D. Language and Linguistics ... 62
  E. Criticism ... 63
  F. Stage History; Productions; Performance Criticism; Film and Television Versions ... 80
  G. Pedagogy ... 87
  H. Bibliographies ... 87

V. *Measure for Measure*
   A. Editions   88
   B. Dating and Textual Studies   90
   C. Influences; Sources; Historical and Intellectual
       Backgrounds; Topicality   90
   D. Language and Linguistics   98
   E. Criticism   98
   F. Stage History; Productions; Performance Criticism;
       Film and Television Versions   117
   G. Adaptations   120
   H. Pedagogy   122
   I. Collections   123
   J. Bibliographies; Concordances; Listings   124

Index I: Authors and Editors (Sections II-V)   125
Index II: Subjects (Sections II-V)   129

PREFACE

The thirteen volumes of this series, of which this is the tenth, are designed to provide a guide to secondary materials on Shakespeare for scholars, graduate and undergraduate students, and college and high school teachers. In ten of the thirteen volumes, entries refer to materials that focus on individual works by Shakespeare; a total of twenty-nine plays, plus *The Rape of Lucrece*, are covered in these volumes. The remaining three volumes present materials that treat Shakespeare in more general ways. These are highly selective bibliographies. While making sure to represent different approaches to the study of Shakespeare, the editors include only work that is either of high quality or of great influence or significance.

In this volume, entries for the works included are numbered consecutively throughout the volume. Within each subsection in Sections III, IV, and V, entries are organized alphabetically by author or editor. Section II, "The Problem Plays as a Group," is short, and therefore its entries have not been divided into subsections. Each entry contains basic factual information and an annotation. Because inclusion of an item in this bibliography implies a positive evaluation, the annotations are primarily descriptive. Occasionally an item—usually an item published early in the twentieth century—will be noted as especially influential or controversial for the scholarship that follows it.

The label "problem play" (sometimes "problem comedy") is itself controversial. Coined at the end of the nineteenth century, the term does not always include the same subset of plays. *Hamlet* is the play most often added to the group, and *Troilus* is sometimes omitted from discussions of the problem plays. Some critics argue vehemently that the term itself has no meaning, that treating a subset of plays under the rubric of "problem" is at best useless and sometimes even misleading. In this volume, *Troilus and Cressida*, *All's Well That Ends Well*, and *Measure for Measure* are "problem plays." Issues particular to each play have resulted in uneven interest among scholars and consequently disproportionate numbers of entries in some categories. For example, the complicated publishing history of *Troilus* means a relatively large number of annotations for that play under the subsection "Dating and Textual Studies," while the controversy over *Measure*'s relationship to the court of King James results in a relatively large number of entries for that play in the subsection "Influences; Sources; Historical and Intellectual Backgrounds; Topicality."

This volume is organized in five sections. Section I, which is essentially the same in all thirteen volumes, contains those editions and general reference works that in the collective opinion of the editors are most basic to the study of Shakespeare. The annotations in this section have been written by the following series editors: Jean E. Howard, Clifford C. Huffman, John S. Mebane, Richard L. Nochimson, Hugh M. Richmond, Barbara H. Traister, and John W. Velz.

Section II contains items that deal with the problem plays as a group or which discuss in relation to one another at least two of the plays treated in this volume. Sections III, IV, and V are subdivided, and the kinds of works collected under each subsection are described in the table of contents. Items that could fit in more than one subsection are cross-referenced by item number at the end of the subsections in which they might also have been included. Items dealing with stage and film productions of these plays are included in the subsections on "Stage History and Performance Criticism." The items included under the subsections on "Adaptations" are works that alter a particular Shakespeare play to produce an independent text with a new title and author.

Within the annotations, parenthetical numbers prefaced by "no." (e.g., no. 47) indicate cross-references to other items in the bibliography; other numbers in parentheses are either page numbers (e.g., 29) or act, scene, and line numbers (e.g., 3.2.1–2) of the passage quoted or discussed. Act, scene, and line numbers are taken from *The Norton Shakespeare* (no. 3).

Abbreviations that appear in the annotations are listed on page xi.

Barbara Howard Traister
Lehigh University

Richard L. Nochimson
Yeshiva University

November 2004

Acknowledgements

The editors wish to thank their families for help and encouragement while compiling this volume. Greatest thanks and credit are due, however, to Dr. Kathleen Mosher, former student and valued friend, who assisted at nearly every stage with this bibliography, searching for and annotating many of the entries for *Measure*, and helping prepare the index. Without her contributions, this volume would have been even longer in process.

Abbreviations

All's Well, AW	*All's Well That Ends Well*
c.	about
chap., chaps.	chapter(s)
ed., eds.	edited by/editor(s)
e.g.	for example
et al.	and others
F1	First Folio
i.e.	that is
Measure, MM	*Measure for Measure*
no., nos.	number(s)
n.s.	new series
p., pp.	page(s)
Q	Quarto
repr.	reprint/reprinted
trans.	translated by
Troilus, TC	*Troilus and Cressida*
Univ.	University
vol., vols.	volume(s)

I. EDITIONS AND REFERENCE WORKS

A. Single-Volume Editions.

1. **Bevington, David,** ed. *The Complete Works of Shakespeare.* 5th edition. New York: Addison Wesley Longman, 2003.

   Bevington's *Complete Works* includes 38 plays and the nondramatic poems. Introductions, aimed at a broad audience, focus upon questions of interpretation, with some attention to performance history. The general introduction discusses social, intellectual, and theatrical history; Shakespeare's biography and his career as a dramatist; his language and versification; editions and editors of Shakespeare; and the history of Shakespearean criticism. Appendices include discussions of canon, dates, and early texts; brief summaries of sources; and performance history. There are genealogical charts, maps, and a selected bibliography. Emendations of the copy text are recorded only in an appendix; they are not bracketed in the texts of the plays, although they are sometimes discussed in the commentary notes that appear at the bottom of each column. Spelling is modernized unless an exception is necessary for scansion, to indicate a pun, or for other reasons discussed in the preface to the updated 4th edition (1997). Notes appear at the bottom of the column. Speech prefixes are expanded. Illustrations include photographs from recent performances. Features ranging from the clarity and high quality of the introductions to the readability of the typeface combine to make the texts in this edition admirably accessible to students and general readers. Available with this edition are the BBC's CD-ROM programs on *Macbeth* and *A Midsummer Night's Dream.* These multimedia resources provide the full text and complete audio recordings; footnotes; word and image searches; sources; comments and audio-visual aids on plot, themes, language, performance history, historical background, and characterization; print capability; and clips from film and video performances. A *Teacher's Guide* to the CD provides suggestions for assignments and classroom use.

2. **Evans, G. Blakemore,** et al., eds. *The Riverside Shakespeare.* 2nd edition. Boston: Houghton Mifflin, 1997.

   This edition includes 39 plays, the nondramatic poems, and segments of *Sir Thomas More*. Introductions by Herschel Baker (histories), Frank Kermode (tragedies), Hallett Smith (romances and nondramatic poems), Anne Barton (comedies), and J. J. M. Tobin ("A Funeral Elegy" by W. S. and *Edward III*) discuss dates, sources, and major interpretive issues. Harry Levin's general introduction discusses Shakespeare's biography, artistic development, and reputation; intellectual backgrounds; Renaissance playhouses and theatrical conventions; Elizabethan English; and stylistic techniques. Heather Dubrow provides an analytical survey of twentieth-century Shakespeare criticism. Evans provides an introduction to textual criticism. Appendices include a history of Shakespearean performance by Charles H. Shattuck and William T. Liston; substantial excerpts from historical documents related to Shakespeare's life and works, including some early responses to the plays; "Annals, 1552–1616," a listing in four parallel columns of events in political history, Shakespeare's biography, theater history, and nondramatic literature; a selected bibliography; indexes; and a glossary. Emendations of the copy text are enclosed in square brackets, and each play is followed by a summary discussion of editorial problems and by textual notes listing the sources of all emendations. Spelling is modernized except for "a selection of Elizabethan spelling forms that reflect ... contemporary pronunciation" (67). Notes appear at the bottom of the column. The volume includes numerous illustrations, including color plates. While the *Riverside* has many features aimed at general readers, the impressive textual apparatus, Evans's fine discussion of textual criticism, and the collection of documents make this edition of special interest to advanced graduate students and to scholars.

3. Greenblatt, Stephen, Walter Cohen, Jean E. Howard, and Katharine Eisaman Maus, eds. *The Norton Shakespeare, Based on the Oxford Edition*. New York: Norton, 1997.

This edition includes 38 plays (including quarto, folio, and conflated texts of *King Lear*) and the nondramatic poems, including works of uncertain authorship not included in other single-volume editions. The texts (except for "A Funeral Elegy," ed. Donald Foster) are updated versions of those in the modern-spelling, single-volume *Oxford Shakespeare* (1988) produced by general editors Stanley Wells and Gary Taylor with John Jowett and William Montgomery. The *Oxford* edition is based on revisionary editorial principles, including the belief that some texts previously regarded as having limited authority are in reality records (at times highly imperfect) of early authorial versions later revised in the theater. The revised versions are usually chosen as control texts. In the *Oxford*, passages from earlier versions are often reprinted in appendices; the *Norton* prints these passages from earlier versions, indented, within the texts. The

Norton Shakespeare provides marginal glosses and numerous explanatory notes; the latter are numbered in the text and appear at the bottom of each page. Textual variants are listed after each work. Stage directions added after the 1623 Folio appear in brackets. Greenblatt's general introduction discusses Renaissance economic, social, religious, and political life; Shakespeare's biography; textual criticism; and aspects of Shakespeare's art, including "The Paradoxes of Identity" in characterization and analysis of the "overpowering exuberance and generosity" (63) of Shakespeare's language. Introductions to individual works discuss a range of historical and aesthetic issues. Appendices include Andrew Gurr's "The Shakespearean Stage"; a collection of documents; a chronicle of events in political and literary history; a bibliography; and a glossary. This edition combines traditional scholarship with a focus on such recent concerns as the status of women and "The English and Otherness." Also available is *The Norton Shakespeare Workshop*, ed. Mark Rose, a set of interactive multimedia programs on CD-ROM that can be purchased either separately or in a package with *The Norton Shakespeare*. The *Workshop* provides searchable texts of *A Midsummer Night's Dream*; *The Merchant of Venice*; *Henry IV, Part Two*; *Othello*; *Hamlet*; *The Tempest*; and Sonnets 55 and 138. Students can find analyses of selected passages, sources, essays that illustrate the play's critical and performance history, clips from classic and from specially commissioned performances, selections of music inspired by the plays, and tools for developing paper topics.

4. Hinman, Charlton, ed. *The Norton Facsimile: The First Folio of Shakespeare*. 2nd edition. Introduction by Peter Blayney. New York: W. W. Norton, 1996.

The First Folio of 1623 is a collection of 36 plays made by Shakespeare's fellow actors, Heminge and Condell. *Pericles*, *The Two Noble Kinsmen*, and the nondramatic poems are not included. Heminge and Condell claim to have provided "perfect" texts, distinguishing them from what they describe as "stolne, and surreptitious copies, maimed, and deformed by the frauds and stealthes of injurious impostors" (A3). While some of the previously published quartos are regarded today as superior versions, the First Folio indeed provides the most authoritative texts for the majority of Shakespeare's plays. It also includes commendatory poems by four authors, including Ben Jonson, and the Droeshout portrait of Shakespeare. During the two years that the 1623 edition was in press, corrections were made continually, and the uncorrected pages became mingled with corrected ones. In addition, imperfections of various sorts render portions of numerous pages difficult or impossible to read. Hinman has examined the 80 copies of the First Folio in the Folger

Shakespeare Library and selected the clearest versions of what appear to be the finally corrected pages. In the left and right margins, he provides for reference his system of "through line numbering," by which he numbers each typographical line throughout the text of a play (the verse and prose of the play as well as all other material such as scene headings and stage directions). In a page from *King John*, for example, which includes what might otherwise be referred to as 3.1.324 through 3.3.74 (this form of reference appears in the bottom margin), the through line numbers run from 1257 to 1380. Appendix A presents some variant states of the Folio text, and Appendix B lists the Folger copies used in compiling this edition. Hinman's introduction discusses the nature and authority of the Folio, the printing and proofreading process, and the procedures followed in editing the facsimile, explaining, among other points, the advantages of through line numbering. Blayney's introduction updates Hinman's discussions of such matters as the status of quarto texts, the types of play-manuscripts available to printers, and the printing and proofreading processes. Blayney also discusses the theory that, since different versions of a given play may represent authorial or collaborative revisions, in such cases there is no "ideal text." No interpretive introductions or glosses are provided. While some valuable facsimiles of quarto versions are available, the Hinman First Folio is clearly an excellent place to begin one's encounter with early printed texts that are not mediated by centuries of editorial tradition.

B. Multi-Volume Editions.

5. Barnet, Sylvan, general ed. *The Signet Classic Shakespeare.* New York: Penguin.

Originally edited in the 1960s, the Signet series was updated in the 1980s; newly revised volumes began to appear in 1998. The 35-volume series includes 38 plays and the nondramatic poems. Collections entitled *Four Great Comedies, Four Great Tragedies,* and *The Sonnets and Nondramatic Poems* are available. Each volume in the newly revised series includes a general introduction with discussions of Shakespeare's biography, including the "anti-Stratfordian" authorship phenomenon; Shakespeare's English; Elizabethan theaters; "Shakespeare's Dramatic Language: Costumes, Gestures and Silences; Prose and Poetry"; editorial principles; and the staging of Shakespeare's plays, including consideration of the concept of the play as a collaboration among the playwright, theatrical ensemble, and audience. Spelling is generally modernized, and speech prefixes are expanded. Explanatory notes appear at the bottom of each page.

Appendices contain textual notes, discussion of (and often excerpts from) sources, several critical essays, a survey of each play's performance history, and a bibliography. Although introductions in this series are written for beginning students, the substantial selection of distinguished critical essays is useful for more advanced students, as well.

6. **Bevington, David,** ed. David Scott Kastan, James Hammersmith, and Robert Kean Turner, associate eds. *The Bantam Shakespeare.* New York: Bantam, 1988.

In 1988, 37 plays and the nondramatic poems were published in the 29 volumes of *The Bantam Shakespeare.* Collections entitled *Four Comedies* and *Four Tragedies* are available. Texts, explanatory notes (at the bottom of each page), and interpretive introductions are similar to those of Bevington's *Complete Works of Shakespeare* (see no. 1). Included in the Bantam series are brief performance histories of individual plays and Joseph Papp's forewords on Shakespeare's enduring appeal. Each volume includes a one-page biography of Shakespeare and an introduction to Elizabethan playhouses. Appendices include concise discussions of dates and early texts, textual notes, substantial excerpts from sources, and a brief annotated bibliography. While this series necessarily excludes some of the historical information found in the *Complete Works,* the forewords by an eminent producer/director and the well-written performance histories are engaging features, especially appropriate for students and general readers.

7. **Brockbank, Philip,** founding general ed. Brian Gibbons, general ed. A. R. Braunmuller, associate general ed. *The New Cambridge Shakespeare.* Cambridge: Cambridge Univ. Press, 1982–.

The New Cambridge series will eventually include 39 plays (with *The Reign of Edward III*) and the nondramatic poems. So far, 43 volumes have appeared; among these are two separate editions (one based on an early quarto) of *King Lear,* of *Hamlet,* of *Othello,* of *Richard III,* and of *Henry V.* Introductions discuss date, sources, critical history and interpretive issues, staging, and performance history (with numerous illustrations). Discussion of the text precedes each play, and more detailed textual analysis sometimes appears in an appendix. All volumes include a selected bibliography. Spelling is generally modernized; speech prefixes are expanded. Textual notes signaling departures from the copy text and extensive explanatory notes appear at the bottom of each page. Designed for students and scholars, *The New Cambridge Shakespeare* provides more detailed attention to stagecraft and performance history than most other editions. This series succeeds *The New Shakespeare,* edited by Arthur Quiller-Couch and John Dover Wilson.

8. Knowles, Richard, and Paul Werstine, general eds. Robert K. Turner, senior consulting editor. *A New Variorum Edition of Shakespeare.* New York: Modern Language Association.

From 1871 to 1928 H. H. Furness, Sr., and H. H. Furness, Jr., published 19 works of the Variorum Shakespeare. Since 1933, nine new editions have appeared in the MLA series. The completed 40-volume variorum will contain 38 plays and the nondramatic poems. Each volume provides an old-spelling text and a collation of significant emendations from previous editions. Explanatory notes (printed below the textual notes at the bottom of each page) try to record all important previous annotation. Appendices include discussions of a play's text and date. Recent volumes survey the history of criticism and performance and refer to a substantial bibliography; early volumes include excerpts from previous criticism. Sources and analogues are discussed and reprinted. As compilations of scholarship, criticism, and textual analysis, these volumes represent a significant resource for scholars and teachers.

9. Mowat, Barbara A., and Paul Werstine, eds. *The New Folger Library Shakespeare.* New York: Pocket Books, Washington Square Press, 1992—.

Twenty-nine volumes of the New Folger series, which replaces *The Folger Library General Reader's Shakespeare,* appeared between 1992 and 2004. Collections entitled *Three Comedies* and *Three Tragedies* are also available. Several new titles will come out each year until the series of 38 plays and the nondramatic poems is complete. Each volume provides a brief initial comment on the play followed by basic introductions to Shakespeare's language and style, his biography, Elizabethan theaters, early editions, and the editorial principles of the series. Half brackets enclose emendations of the copy text; in some volumes square or pointed brackets indicate the sources of passages that appear (for example) only in the folio or an earlier quarto. Explanatory notes appear on pages facing the text, textual notes in an appendix. Spelling is selectively modernized, and speech prefixes are expanded. For each play a different critic offers the "Modern Perspective" that follows the text. A brief annotated bibliography focuses mostly on recent approaches to the play; standard works on language, biography, theatrical setting, and early texts also appear. While this series aims at the broadest possible audience, the clarity and helpfulness of its introductions and explanatory notes make it especially well suited for beginning students.

10. Proudfoot, Richard, Ann Thompson, and David Scott Kastan, general eds. George Walton Williams, associate general ed. *The Arden Shakespeare.* London, U.K.: Thomson Learning.

EDITIONS AND REFERENCE WORKS 7

The 40-volume *Arden Shakespeare* includes 38 plays and 2 volumes of the nondramatic poems. The edition is continually updated; although some current volumes are from the 1950s, nineteen plays and the Sonnets have appeared in revised third editions in recent years. Introductions provide extensive discussion of dates, texts, editorial principles, sources, and a wide range of interpretive issues. Extensive textual and explanatory notes appear at the bottom of each page. Appendices typically include additional textual analysis, excerpts from sources, and (sometimes) settings for songs. The Arden series often includes scholarship and criticism that are essential for advanced students and scholars. The complete second edition of the Arden series is available on CD-ROM from Primary Source Media. The CD-ROMs enable one to view the edited texts simultaneously with materials from the following: early quarto and folio editions; Bullough's *Narrative and Dramatic Sources* (no. 15); Abbott's *Shakespearian Grammar*; Onions's *Shakespeare Glossary* (no. 23); Partridge's *Shakespeare's Bawdy*; and a 4,600-item bibliography. The complete Arden set is also available on-line, with additional materials for those works that have appeared in the third edition.

11. Spencer, T. J. B., founding general ed. Stanley Wells, associate ed. *The New Penguin Shakespeare*. London: Penguin Books.

The 40-volume New Penguin series now includes 37 plays and the nondramatic poems; *Cymbeline* is planned. Dates range from the 1960s through 2001. Introductions discuss a range of interpretive issues and are followed by brief bibliographical essays. Explanatory notes follow the text, succeeded by textual analysis, selective textual notes, and (as appropriate) settings for songs. Spelling is modernized, and speech prefixes are expanded. Emendations of the copy text are not bracketed. The New Penguin will appeal especially to those who wish the pages of the text to be free of annotation.

12. Wells, Stanley, general ed. Advisory eds. S. Schoenbaum, G. R. Proudfoot, and F. W. Sternfeld. *The Oxford Shakespeare*. Oxford: Oxford Univ. Press.

Between 1982 and 2004, 31 plays and *Shakespeare: The Complete Sonnets and Poems* were published in the multi-volume *Oxford Shakespeare*. The completed series will include 38 plays and the nondramatic poems. Introductions provide detailed discussion of dates, sources, textual criticism, questions of interpretation, and performance history. Textual notes and extensive commentary appear at the bottom of each page. The commentary and introduction are indexed. Spelling is modernized, and speech prefixes are expanded. The Oxford series is based on revisionary editorial principles, including the belief that some texts previously regarded as of little value are in reality records (at times highly imperfect) of early authorial versions later revised in the theater. The revised versions are usually chosen as copy texts, and appendices sometimes include passages from earlier printed versions. Some appendices include musical settings for songs. Partly because of its editorial principles, this series is of special interest to scholars and advanced students.

C. Basic Reference Works for Shakespeare Studies.

13. Beckerman, Bernard. *Shakespeare at the Globe: 1599–1609.* New York: Macmillan, 1962.

This study of the 29 extant plays (including 15 by Shakespeare) produced at the Globe in its first decade yields information about the playhouse and how Shakespeare's company performed in it. The first chapter, on the repertory system, is based on analysis of Henslowe's diary. Subsequent chapters about the stage itself, acting styles, the dramatic form of plays and of scenes within plays, and the staging derive from study of the Globe repertory. Detailed appendices provide statistics on which Beckerman's analysis partly depends. Beckerman concludes that the style in which these plays were presented was neither symbolic nor what modern audiences would call realistic. Rather, he suggests, passion by the actors was presented within a framework of staging and scenic conventions in various styles according to the needs of particular plays.

14. Bentley, G. E. *The Jacobean and Caroline Stage.* 7 vols. Oxford: Clarendon Press, 1941–68.

Bentley designed his survey of British drama to carry on that of Chambers (see no. 16) and cover the years 1616–42. The 11 chapters in vol. 1 provide detailed information about 11 adult and children's acting companies (1–342); vol. 2 surveys information about actors, listed alphabetically (343–629), with relevant documents reprinted and annotated (630–96), with an index (697–748). Vols. 3, 4, 5 are an alphabetical list, by author, with bibliographical material and commentary, of "all plays, masques, shows, and dramatic entertainments which were written or first performed in England between 1616 ... and ... 1642" (3.v), from "M.A." to Richard Zouche, with a final section (5. 1281–1456) on anonymous and untitled plays. Vol. 6 considers theater buildings (private, 3–117; public, 121–252; court, 255–88; and two that were only projected, 291–309). Vol. 7 gathers together, as appendices to vol. 6, "scattered material concerning Lenten performances and Sunday performances" and arranges chronologically "a large number of dramatic and semi-dramatic events" of interest to students of dramatic literature and theater history (6.v); it includes a general index for vols. 1-7 (129-390) which has numerous references (344-45) to Shakespeare and his plays.

15. Bullough, Geoffrey. *Narrative and Dramatic Sources of Shakespeare.* 8 vols. London and New York: Routledge & Kegan Paul and Columbia Univ. Press, 1957-75.

This work is a comprehensive compendium of the texts of Shakespeare's sources for 37 plays and several poems. Bullough includes analogues as well as sources and "possible sources" as well as "probable sources." All texts are in English, old-spelling Elizabethan when extant, and in some other cases in the compiler's translation. Bullough includes a separate introduction for each play. In the early volumes, interpretation is largely left to the reader; introductions in the later volumes include more interpretation and tend to be longer. There have been complaints of occasional errors in transcription. The major caveat, however, about using this learned, thorough, and imaginative work concerns what Bullough could not conceivably print: the passages in his sources that Shakespeare presumably read but either chose to omit or neglected to include.

16. Chambers, E. K. *The Elizabethan Stage.* 4 vols. Oxford: Clarendon Press, 1923. Revised 1945; with corrections 1967.

In vol. 1, Chambers provides detailed information about the court (1-234): the monarchs, their households, the Revels Office, pageantry, the mask, and the court play. In the section entitled "The Control of the Stage" (236-388), he covers the struggles between the city of London and the court and between Humanism and Puritanism, and treats the status of actors and the socio-economic realities of actors' lives. In vol. 2, Chambers focuses on the history of 38 different acting companies (children, adult, and foreign) (1-294), gives details, such as are known, about an alphabetical list of actors (295-350), and treats the playhouses (16 public and 2 private theaters), including discussion of their structure and management (351-557). In vol. 3, Chambers surveys the conditions of staging in the court and theaters (1-154), the printing of plays (157-200), and then offers a bibliographical survey, including brief biographies, of playwrights alphabetically arranged, from William Alabaster through Christopher Yelverton (201-518). In vol. 4, Chambers concludes that bibliography with anonymous work (1-74) and presents 13 appendices that reprint or summarize relevant historical documents. Chambers concludes this work with four indices (to plays, persons, places, and subjects) to the four volumes (409-67). In these four volumes, Chambers presents an encyclopedia of all aspects of English drama during the reigns of Elizabeth I and James I up to the date of Shakespeare's death in 1616. A subsequent and detailed index to this entire work was compiled by Beatrice White, *An Index to "The Elizabethan Stage" and "William Shakespeare" by Sir Edmund Chambers*. Oxford: Oxford Univ. Press, 1934.

17. Chambers, E. K. *William Shakespeare: A Study of Facts and Problems.* 2 vols. Oxford: Clarendon Press, 1930. Repr., 1931.

This work is an encyclopedia of information relating to Shakespeare. The principal topics of the first volume are the dramatist's family origins, his relations to the theater and its professionals, the nature of the texts of his plays—including their preparation for performance and publication, and also questions of authenticity and chronology (relevant tables about the quartos and metrics are in the second volume). The data available (and plausible conjectures) concerning all texts attributed to Shakespeare, including poems and uncertain attributions, are then laid out title by title. The second volume cites the significant Shakespeare records then available, including contemporary allusions, performance data, legends, and even forgeries (the last two items are more fully covered in Schoenbaum's *Shakespeare's Lives*). There are comprehensive indices and a substantial bibliography. While it is sometimes necessary to update this book by correlation with Schoenbaum's *Documentary Life* (see no. 25) and other, more recent, texts, Chambers's scholarship has been supplemented rather than invalidated by more recent research, and his work remains a convenient starting point for pursuit of background data on Shakespeare's life and works.

18. De Grazia, Margreta, and Stanley Wells, eds. *The Cambridge Companion to Shakespeare*. Cambridge: Cambridge Univ. Press, 2001.

Following a preface, a "partial chronology" of Shakespeare's life and a "conjectural" one of his works, the nineteen chapters of this new edition of the *Cambridge Companion* (the others were 1934, 1971, and 1986) provide a "broadly historical or cultural approach" instead of the earlier volumes' "formalist orientation" (xv). Ernst Honigmann writes on Shakespeare's life (chap. 1), Barbara A. Mowat discusses the traditions of editing (chap. 2, an essay supplemented by Michael Dobson's survey of page- or stage-oriented editions, chap. 15), Leonard Barkan reviews what Shakespeare read (chap. 3), and Margreta De Grazia skims over some aspects of language and rhetoric (chap. 4). John Kerrigan is specific in his discussion of the poems (chap. 5), a specificity balanced by the more general essays of Susan Snyder on the possibilities of genre (chap. 6), Valerie

Traub on Shakespeare's use of gender and sexuality (chap. 9), and David Scott Kastan on the use of history (chap. 11). Social baackground—the City, Court, Playhouse, etc.—are the subjects of chapters by John H. Astington and Anne Barton (chaps. 7, 8), and Ania Loomba goes farther afield in spotlighting "outsiders" in England and Shakespeare (chap. 10). The last chapters group into two divisions: Shakespeare's posthumous presence in the (British) theater of 1660–1900 (Lois Potter, chap. 12) and in that of the 20th century (Peter Holland, chap. 13), in the cinema (Russell Jackson, chap. 14), on stages and pages worldwide (Dennis Kennedy, chap. 16); and, second, the history of Shakespeare criticism (1600–1900 by Hugh Grady, chap. 17; 1900–2000 by R. S. White, chap. 18). The volume concludes with an annotated list of Shakespeare reference books recommended by Dieter Mehl (chap. 19). Each essay except the last appends its own (further) reading list.

This volume does not precisely replace its immediate predecessor (ed. Wells, 1986, repr. 1991), for the latter's "basic materials ... on Shakespeare's life, ... the transmission of the text, and the history of both criticism and production are still [fortunately] available" (xvi). This availability does not prevent the present volume from printing new essays on some of the same topics; and students, teachers, and scholars may well benefit from comparing the generations—for instance Ernst Honigmann with S. Schoenbaum on Shakespeare's biography, Margreta De Grazia with Inga-Stina Ewbank on Shakespeare and language, Russell Jackson with Robert Hapgood on film (and, in the earlier edition, television) versions of Shakespeare, Hugh Grady with Harry Levin on Shakespeare criticism to about 1900, and R. S. White with the three scholars who wrote three separate essays on his topic, 20th-century Shakespeare criticism. The 1986 edition, then, should be consulted in addition to this new entry.

19. Doran, Madeleine. *Endeavors of Art: A Study of Form in Elizabethan Drama.* Madison: Univ. of Wisconsin Press, 1954.

Doran reconstructs the Elizabethan assumptions about many aspects of dramatic form, defined broadly enough to include genre, eloquence and copiousness, character, and "moral aim." A detailed exploration of classical, medieval, and Renaissance backgrounds makes this a study in historical criticism; however, the cultural context laid out is aesthetic, not ideational. Doran examines the problems of form faced by Shakespeare and his contemporaries—problems of genre, of character, of plot construction—in an attempt to explain the success (or, sometimes, lack of success) of the major dramatists in "achieving form adequate to meaning" (23). Doran's unpretentious, readable study is justly famous as the first book on the aesthetics of Renaissance drama to understand the entire context, to perceive the Renaissance assumptions about dramatic art as a fusion of classical and medieval influences.

20. Gurr, Andrew. *Playgoing in Shakespeare's London.* 2nd edition. Cambridge: Cambridge Univ. Press, 1996.

Gurr focuses on the identity, class, and changing tastes of London playgoers from the opening of the Red Lion in 1567 to the closing of the theaters in 1642. He examines the locations, physical features, price scales, and repertories of the various playhouses, distinguishing particularly between "halls" and "amphitheatres" and rejecting the more common labels "private" and "public." Turning from the theaters, Gurr examines the playgoers, asking such questions as whether they ventured to the playhouses primarily to "hear" a text or to "see" a spectacle. In a final chapter, entitled "The evolution of tastes," he discusses assorted playgoing fashions: from the craze for Tarlton's clowning to the taste for pastoral and romance in the last years of Charles I. Two appendices list identifiable playgoers and references to playgoing during the time period.

21. Gurr, Andrew. *The Shakespearean Stage 1574–1642.* 3rd edition. Cambridge: Cambridge Univ. Press, 1992.

Gurr summarizes a vast amount of scholarship concerning the material conditions of Elizabethan, Jacobean, and Caroline theatrical production. Each of his six chapters provides a wealth of detailed information on theatrical life. The first gives an overview of the place of the theater in urban London from the 1570s until 1642, including an examination of the social status of playwrights, the differences and similarities between the repertories at the open-air amphitheaters (public) and at the indoor playhouses (private), and the changing role of court patronage of theater. Chapter two describes the typical composition of London theater companies and their regulation by the Crown. It also gives an historical account of the theatrical companies that at various times dominated the London theatrical scene. In his third chapter, Gurr looks at actors, discussing the famous clowns of the Elizabethan era, prominent tragic actors such as Burbage and Alleyn, and the repertory system within which they worked. The fourth chapter summarizes what is known about the playhouses, including information gleaned from the recent excavation of the remains of the Rose Theater, as well as accounts of the Globe Theater, The Fortune, the hall playhouses, and the Banqueting Hall. Chapter five discusses staging conventions and the differences between public and private theaters, and among the various particular theaters, in their use of song, music, clowning, and jigging. Also examined are stage properties and costumes. The final chapter analyzes information about audiences: who went to which kinds of playhouse and how they behaved. Gurr argues that women and all social classes were represented in theatrical audiences, with an increasing tendency in the seventeenth century for the private theaters to cater to a wealthier clientele who demanded a more sophisticated repertory with more new plays. This valuable book concludes with an appendix indicating at which playhouses and by which companies various plays were staged.

22. Kastan, David Scott, ed. *A Companion to Shakespeare.* Oxford: Blackwell Publishers, 1999.

This collection of 28 essays, most with notes and references for further reading, aims to locate Shakespeare in relation to the historical matrix in which he wrote his plays and poems. Following the editor's introduction, the volume is framed by two essays dealing with Shakespeare the man. The first, by David Bevington, deals with what is known, factually, about his life; the last, by Michael Bristol, deals with various myths surrounding the figure of Shakespeare. In between, the book is divided into five sections. The first contains six essays, mainly by historians, dealing with Shakespeare's England, the city of London, religious identities of the period, the family and household structures, Shakespeare and political thought, and the political culture of the Tudor–Stuart period. The second section contains five essays, mostly by literary critics, and discusses readers and reading practices in the early modern period. It includes a general essay on literacy, illiteracy, and reading practices, and four essays focusing on reading, respectively, the Bible, the classics, historical writings, and vernacular literature. The third part of the book deals with writing and writing practices and contains five essays by literary scholars on writing plays, on the state of the English language in Shakespeare's day, on technical aspects of Shakespeare's dramatic verse, on the rhetorical culture of the times, and on genre. These essays are followed by a section on playing and performance. It contains five essays, mostly by theater historians, on the economics of playing, on The Chamberlain's-King's Men, on Shakespeare's repertory, on playhouses of the day, and on licensing and censorship. The final section, consisting of five essays by literary critics, deals with aspects of printing and print culture, including Shakespeare's works in print between 1593 and 1640, manuscript playbooks, the craft of printing, the London book trade, and press censorship. Mixing traditional and newer topics and concerns, *A Companion to Shakespeare* is an up-to-date guide to the historical conditions and the literary and theatrical resources enabling Shakespeare's art.

23. Onions, C. T. *A Shakespeare Glossary.* Oxford: Clarendon Press, 1911. 2nd edition revised, 1919. Repr., with corrections, 1946; with enlarged Addenda, 1958. Enlarged and revised by Robert D. Eagleson, 1986; corrected, 1988.

Onions's dictionary of Elizabethan vocabulary as it applies to Shakespeare was an offshoot of his work on the *Oxford English Dictionary.* Eagleson updates the third edition with new entries, using modern research (now aided by citations from the Riverside edition [see no. 2], keyed by the Spevack *Concordance* [see no. 26]), while conserving much from Onions's adaptation of *OED* entries to distinguish Shakespearean uses from those of his contemporaries and from modern standard meanings. The glossary covers only expressions that differ from modern usage, as with "cousin" or "noise." It includes some proper names with distinctive associations, such as "Machiavel," and explains unfamiliar stage directions: "sennet" (a trumpet signal). Many allusions are more fully elucidated, as with the origin of "hobby-horse" in morris dances, or the bearing of "wayward" on *Macbeth*'s "weird sisters." This text, which demonstrates the importance of historical awareness of language for accuracy in the close reading of Shakespeare, now has a brief bibliography of relevant texts. It still needs to be supplemented in two areas: information about definite and possible sexual significance of many common and obscure words appears in Gordon Williams' 3-volume *A Dictionary of Sexual Language and Imagery in Shakespearean and Stuart Literature* (1994); often contradictory guidance about the likely pronunciation of Shakespeare's language is provided by Helge Kökeritz's *Shakespeare's Pronunciation* (1953) and by Fausto Cercignani's *Shakespeare's Works and Elizabethan Pronunciation* (1981).

24. Rothwell, Kenneth S., and Annabelle Henkin Melzer. *Shakespeare on Screen: An International Filmography and Videography.* New York: Neal-Schuman, 1990.

This list of film and video versions of Shakespeare seeks to be comprehensive, covering the years 1899–1989, except that it excludes most silent films, referring the reader to Robert Hamilton Ball's *Shakespeare on Silent Film* (1968). It does include "modernizations, spinoffs, musical and dance versions, abridgements, travesties and excerpts" (x). The introduction, by Rothwell, offers an overview of screen versions of Shakespeare (1–17). The body of the work, with over 675 entries (21–316), is organized by play, listed alphabetically, and within each play chronologically. Represented are 37 plays and the *Sonnets*. *Pericles* and *Timon of Athens* appear only in the BBC versions in "The Shakespeare Plays" series. For *Hamlet* we have 87 entries. Included also are another 74 entries (317–35) for documentaries and other "unclassifiable" films and videos that present Shakespeare in some form, such as John Barton's "Playing Shakespeare" series and James Ivory's film, "Shakespeare Wallah." The sometimes quite extensive entries include information about and evaluation of the production, and an attempt to provide information about distribution and availability. The work concludes with a useful selected bibliography with brief annotations (337–45), a series of helpful indices (349–98), and a list of the names and addresses of distributors, dealers, and archives (399–404). Also valuable is Rothwell's *A History of Shakespeare on Screen* (Cambridge Univ. Press, 2004), a comprehensive study of the subject which contains an abbreviated filmography.

25. Schoenbaum, S. *William Shakespeare: A Compact Documentary Life.* Oxford: Oxford Univ. Press, 1977. Repr., with corrections, 1978.

An abridged version of Schoenbaum's massive documentary study of Shakespeare published by Oxford in 1975, the *Compact Documentary Life* traces all textual evidence about Shakespeare chronologically from his grandfather's generation up to the deaths of Shakespeare's surviving family members. Legends for which there is no specific documentation—such as the deer-poaching incident—are examined for probability on the basis of surviving materials. Where appropriate, Schoenbaum juxtaposes biographical details with specific passages in Shakespeare's works. Amply illustrated and annotated, this work, unlike Schoenbaum's earlier, larger version and his later (1981) *William Shakespeare: Records and Images*, refers to documents but generally does not reprint them.

26. Spevack, Marvin. *The Harvard Concordance to Shakespeare.* Cambridge: Belknap Press of Harvard Univ. Press, 1973.

This text covers the total of 29,066 words (including proper names) used by Shakespeare in his plays and poems, in the modern-spelling text of *The Riverside Shakespeare* (see no. 2). Stage directions appear in another volume. Contexts are omitted for the first 43 words in order of frequency, mostly pronouns, prepositions, conjunctions, auxiliary verbs, and articles. Individual entries distinguish between prose and verse, and between total and relative frequencies. The modern spelling is not enforced with proper names or significant Elizabethan divergencies: "embassador-ambassador." While the cited context of each use is normally the line of text in which it appears, other limits occur when the sense requires further wording. This concordance helps to locate specific passages and also invites subtler research uses, such as study of the recurrence of words in each play: thus the continuity of *Henry VIII* from *Richard III* appears in their shared distinctive use of certain religious terms. Similarly, accumulated references show the divergence or consistency of meaning or associations for particular terms (Shakespeare's references to dogs are unfavorable). In using this text, one must remember that variant spellings or forms of speech may conceal recurrences of words with the same root or meaning (guilt, gilt, guilts, guilty, guiltily, guiltless), while similar spellings of the same word may have contrasting senses (your grace [the Duke] of York, the grace of God, external grace). The provided contexts reveal the complications, but often are too brief to ensure exact interpretation of a word. The magnitude of the effort involved in this concordance indicates the research gain from electronic procedures, which also permit many permutations of its data, as seen in the nine volumes of Spevack's *A Complete and Systematic Concordance to the Works of Shakespeare* (1968–80).

27. Styan, J. L. *Shakespeare's Stagecraft.* Cambridge: Cambridge Univ. Press, 1967. Repr., with corrections, 1971.

Styan's book explores how Shakespeare's plays would have worked, theatrically, on the Elizabethan stage. Beginning with a discussion of the kind of stage for which Shakespeare wrote and of the conventions of performance that obtained on that stage, Styan then devotes the bulk of his attention to Shakespeare's handling of the visual and aural dimensions of performance. He argues that the scripts guide actors in communicating aurally, visually, and kinetically with an audience. Topics considered include gesture, entrances and exits, the use of downstage and upstage playing areas, eavesdropping encounters, the visual orchestration of scenes involving one or several or many characters, the manipulation of rhythm and tempo, and variations among stage voices. The final chapter, "Total Theater," discusses the inseparability of all the elements of Shakespeare's stagecraft in the shaping of a theatrical event aimed at provoking and engaging the audience's fullest response. The book makes a strong case for studying Shakespeare's plays as flexible blueprints for performance that skillfully utilize and transform the stagecraft conventions of the Elizabethan theater.

Note on Bibliographies

In addition to the above works, readers should be aware of the various bibliographies of Shakespeare studies. Among the most valuable are Stanley Wells, *Shakespeare: A Bibliographical Guide*, Oxford: Clarendon Press, 1990; David M. Bergeron and Geraldo U. De Sousa, *Shakespeare: A Study and Research Guide*, 3rd edition, Lawrence: Univ. Press of Kansas, 1995;

Larry S. Champion, *The Essential Shakespeare: An Annotated Bibliography of Major Modern Studies*, 2nd edition, New York: Hall, 1993. Thorough bibliographies for each of a gradually increasing number of plays have been appearing since 1980 in the Garland Shakespeare Bibliographies, general editor William L. Godshalk. An important specialized bibliography is John W. Velz, *Shakespeare and the Classical Tradition: A Critical Guide to Commentary, 1660–1960*, Minneapolis: Univ. of Minnesota Press, 1968 (available on-line). In the special area of Shakespearean pedagogy, a useful (although brief) bibliography appears in Peggy O'Brien, "'And Gladly Teach': Books, Articles, and a Bibliography on the Teaching of Shakespeare," *Shakespeare Quarterly* 46 (1995): 165–72. For information on new materials on the study of Shakespeare, readers should consult the annual bibliographies published by *Shakespeare Quarterly* (*World Shakespeare Bibliography*, also available on line), *PMLA* (*The MLA International Bibliography*, also available on-line and on CD-ROM), the Modern Humanities Research Association (*Annual Bibliography of English Language and Literature*, available on-line), and the English Association (*The Year's Work in English Studies*). Ph.D. theses on Shakespeare are listed in *Dissertation Abstracts International*, which is also available on-line.

II. PROBLEM PLAYS AS A GROUP

28. Bevington, David, ed., David Scott Kastan, James Hammersmith, and Robert Kean Turner, associate eds. *Measure for Measure, All's Well That Ends Well, Troilus and Cressida.* The Bantam Shakespeare. New York: Bantam Books, 1988.

In common with the other editions in this series (see no. 6), a single-page biographical sketch of Shakespeare and information on the playhouse, including the 1596 de Witt drawing of the Swan Theatre, are included in the prefatory materials. Joseph Papp's foreword stresses the accessibility of Shakespearean language and the primacy of performance experience. A brief essay introduces the modern grouping of these works as "problem plays"; a similarly brief introduction to *Measure* familiarizes readers with the moral and social problems appearing in the play and the responses of its main characters. A relatively detailed stage history precedes each text, which is followed by concise notes on date and copy text, textual notes, and a discussion of sources.

29. Boas, Frederick S. *Shakspere and his Predecessors*, 344-84. London: John Murray, 1896.

Boas is the first critic to use the term "problem plays" (among which he includes *Hamlet*) to refer to a subset of Shakespeare's plays. He associates the dark tone of these plays with some unknown change in Shakespeare's life and characterizes them as having "highly artificial societies, whose civilization is ripe unto rottenness" (345) and unsatisfying outcomes. He comments separately on each play, paying special attention to the heroines. Helena, whom he reads as attempting to save Bertram from himself, he deems "a trifle *bourgeoise*"(352), worthy of audience admiration but not of their love. To Isabella he gives highest praise, seeing her in her projected role as Vincentio's wife as a "saviour of society" (369). Cressida, he believes, is a "shallow wanton" who destroys Troilus, the "heroic greenhorn" (374). Boas looks in some detail at *Troilus*'s classical and medieval sources to argue that the play is a parody of the medieval versions of the Trojan War, a "satire of chivalry" (383).

30. Evans, Gareth Lloyd. "Directing Problem Plays: John Barton Talks to Gareth Lloyd Evans." *Shakespeare Survey* 25 (1972): 63-71.

Written as a question and answer interview, the article reveals that, having directed all three problem plays, Barton does not find the label useful. Barton sees *Troilus* as a profounder and richer play than either *All's Well* or *Measure*. He also believes that the second half of the twentieth century was more receptive than earlier periods to satiric, dark plays like *Troilus*. As a director he rejects symbolic or allegorical readings of plays because he needs the characters to come to life on stage. Barton claims that the split which critics often note in *Measure* dissolves in the theater. Particular moments in Barton's productions are discussed: Isabella's refusal to make up her mind about the Duke's proposal; Bertram's final position in *All's Well*; Ajax's expression of sympathy for Hector's death. Evans asks Barton to compare his conception of *All's Well* to Tyrone Guthrie's production of the play and to compare Thersites (*Troilus*) and Lavache (*All's Well*) as indicators of difference among the problem plays. Finally, Barton speaks of the impossibility, in the theater, of leaving options open: actors must decide what their characters mean. And he addresses the difference between dealing with plays as an academic critic and as a director.

31. Foakes, R. A. *Shakespeare: The Dark Comedies to the Last Plays, from Satire to Celebration*, 1–62. Charlottesville: Univ. of Virginia, 1971.

Foakes looks at the last plays as designed for performance. As a prelude to discussion of the romances, he examines what he calls the "dark comedies" and their links to newly-fashionable satiric drama. *All's Well* he reads as having a jarring edge, a romantic comedy modified by a strain of action which shows the intractable nature of things as they are. For Foakes, its tone is set by the sardonic Parolles and Lafew. Similarly in *Measure*, Lucio and Pompey appear early to establish tone. In contrast to their linguistic and moral flexibility, Foakes notes the rigidity of Angelo and Isabella and suggests that it is the urge to live, not the resolve to die, which carries the play's action. All three final marriages, according to Foakes, are a way of recovering health after punishment and expiation, though he thinks *Measure* an unbalanced play. *Troilus* he associates closely with the new satiric comedy of Jonson and Marston, noting that satiric detachment marks the play. In all three plays Foakes finds the heroines contradictory and perverse and the heroes shrunk in comparison to their counterparts in the romantic comedies.

32. Frye, Northrop. *The Myth of Deliverance: Reflections on Shakespeare's Problem Comedies*. Toronto: Univ. of Toronto Press, 1983.

Frye disclaims from the opening pages the idea that the problem plays are more serious or realistic than Shakespeare's romantic comedies. Calling them chiefly "retellings of folk tales" (4), Frye reads these plays—borrowing terminology for structural analyses from Aristotle and Plato—as a series of reversals. *Measure* he terms a "dramatic diptych" (24) in which the original tragic action is abruptly reversed into comedy. In *All's Well*, Frye discerns a thematic reversal (what he calls a reversal of energy) as the older characters who open the play talking of death are replaced by a rejuvenated King and, in the final scene, by a pregnant Helena. *Troilus*, on the other hand, withholds the deliverance Frye finds in the other two plays, reflecting instead a society in need of deliverance: "Being disillusioned with a world like that is the starting point of any genuine myth of deliverance" (85). Throughout these printed lectures (no footnotes), Frye reads the problem comedies as precursors of the romances and applies his usual analysis of mythic structures.

33. **Lawrence, William Witherle.** *Shakespeare's Problem Comedies.* New York: Macmillan, 1931.

Adopting the phrase "problem plays" from F. S. Boas (see no. 29), Lawrence defines these plays as offering realistic and serious treatment of a distressing complication in human life, but without a tragic conclusion. Lawrence devotes individual chapters to *All's Well, Measure,* and *Troilus,* as well as one to the wager plot in *Cymbeline*. Though he views *All's Well* as flawed, Lawrence argues that Renaissance audiences' familiarity with folk tale analogues would have made them more accepting of the play's action than are modern audiences. *Measure* is read as a somewhat unsuccessful mixture of two styles—realism (as seen in Claudio, Angelo, and Isabella) and folk motifs (as seen in the Duke and Mariana). Lawrence discusses the changing views of the *Troilus* story and attributes that play's dissonances to the differences in the play's two plots: the philosophical military debates and the love story. Lawrence concludes that the problem plays differ from the earlier comedies primarily in their preoccupation with the darker side of life. He argues vigorously against the critical view that these plays can be connected to gloom in Shakespeare's own life by pointing out a similar tone in the work of many of Shakespeare's contemporaries.

34. **Leonard, Nancy S.** "Substitution in Shakespeare's Problem Comedies." *English Literary Renaissance* 9 (1979): 281-301.

Leonard believes that the three plays have as a generic link the ambiguities of uncertain judgment, a theme Shakespeare presents by stressing the act of substitution. In *Troilus*, Ajax substitutes for Achilles while Troilus creates a substitute Cressida who is not "Diomed's Cressida." In *All's Well*, Helena substitutes for Diana in Bertram's bed. In *Measure*, the Duke, Angelo, Isabella, and Mariana all play substitute roles. Leonard concludes that Shakespeare uses the uncertainty created by substitution to unsettle the comic form and to deny a sense of closure.

35. McCandless, David. *Gender and Performance in Shakespeare's Problem Comedies.* Bloomington: Indiana Univ. Press, 1997.

McCandless suggests that the problem comedies dramatize a crisis in gender which he associates with the final years of a dominant, unmarried Queen and the accession of a retiring, sybaritic King. In his monograph, McCandless combines feminist and psychoanalytic analysis with performance suggestions for contemporary stagings of each of the problem plays, calling them Brechtian *gesti* that foreground the gender issues he believes the plays embody. In *All's Well*, he suggests staging the bed-trick to "accentuate the tension between Helena's aggressive sexuality and her self-abasing hyper-femininity in order to underscore her status as undecipherable conundrum" (23). In *Measure*, a play he finds filled with masochism and sadism, he once staged Angelo's threats against Isabella as an attempted rape, a physical assault which Claudio unwittingly mimicked as he pleaded with her for his life. McCandless thus tried to make his audience understand Isabella's insistence on her chastity. In *Troilus*, he proposes staging a "fragmented" Cressida whose multiple costumes and attitudes signify a "sequence of adaptations to imposed images of femininity" (148). McCandless characterizes these three plays as "provocative interrogation of erotic politics" which "expose the representational limits of a phallocentric economy of meaning" (166). Imagining "gestic stagings," he believes, can bring about understanding of the plays' "critique of the sex-gender system" (166).

36. Muir, Kenneth, and Stanley Wells, eds. *Aspects of Shakespeare's "Problem Plays."* Cambridge: Cambridge Univ. Press, 1982.

This volume brings together critical articles reprinted from *Shakespeare Survey* volumes from the 1950s though the 1970s which deal with *All's Well*, *Troilus*, and *Measure*. The collection begins with an interview with John Barton (see no. 30) and continues with three articles on *All's Well*, three on *Measure*, and two on *Troilus*. The critical articles are followed by Michael Jamieson's "The Problem Plays, 1920–1970: A Retrospective," in which he surveys their critical reception. The volume concludes with reviews of eight productions of the plays, two from the Old Vic theater and the remainder Stratford-upon-Avon productions. These range from the Old Vic's 1953 *All's Well* to a 1978 *Measure* from Stratford. The volume is illustrated with black and white photographs of twentieth-century productions of the plays.

37. Righter, Anne. *Shakespeare and the Idea of the Play*, 172–83. London: Chatto & Windus, 1965.

Righter's book examines the way the theater is presented in Shakespeare's plays. In a section entitled "Dark Comedies and 'Troilus,'" she explores the darkening of tone and the cynicism which appear in drama written after 1600. With regard to the three plays with which this bibliography deals, Righter argues that "acting" and theatrical metaphors are associated with hollow pretension and pride. She asserts that reality is too complex for human playwrights, like the Duke in *Measure*, to attempt to script other people's lives.

38. Thomas, Vivian. *The Moral Universe of Shakespeare's Problem Plays*. Totowa, NJ: Barnes & Noble, 1987.

In a brief introduction, Thomas surveys the use of the term "problem plays" by critics from Dowden to Northrop Frye (no. 32) and then lists "connecting links" (14) which support the grouping of *All's Well*, *Measure*, and *Troilus*. In his second chapter, Thomas surveys the major sources of the three plays, with special attention to the sources of *Troilus*, and the innovations Shakespeare made in his version of each story. In a chapter devoted to *Troilus*, Thomas focuses on three elements—the "pattern of division" (82) or fragmentation in the play, its concern with the nature of human identity, and its imagery. The chapter concludes with a brief discussion of the Royal Shakespeare Company's 1988 production in Stratford (135–36). Thomas's discussion of *All's Well* deals primarily with Bertram, whom he calls a "nasty little egoist" (167), and the issues of virtue and honor. He concludes that the play has two endings, the fairy tale and the realistic, and that audiences are torn over which to accept. His chapter on *Measure* deals with the pressures put on Angelo and Isabella, personal and social, and with the Duke, the representative of authority and order properly tempered by mercy, who wishes to test them. In his concluding chapter, Thomas addresses the "space" (212) between *Troilus* and the two comedies by looking once more at their similarities, most centrally their exploration of individual and social values. He concludes "the problem plays articulate the problems but don't attempt to solve them" (230).

39. Tillyard, E. M. W. *Shakespeare's Problem Plays*. The Alexander Lectures. Toronto: Univ. of Toronto Press, 1950.

Tillyard provides four chapters, each focused on one "problem play" [*Hamlet* is added to the three treated in this volume]. Speculative thinking, interest in the workings of the human mind, and a reflection of real life characterize these plays, Tillyard argues. He then summarizes and comments on each play. *Troilus* is derived from the medieval conception of the Trojan War, he says, especially from Lydgate's. The Trojans are emotional and old-fashioned; the Greeks are rational and modern with Time on their side, he concludes; and Ulysses and Troilus lead (and best represent) their respective sides. Tillyard sees *Troilus* as a successful play; *All's Well* and *Measure* he dubs interesting failures. Praising the plot construction and characterization of *All's Well*, Tillyard finds in its language a failure of the poetic imagination. *Measure* falters, he claims, when Shakespeare changes styles in 3.1, lowering the "poetical tension" (124). Isabella's character shifts at this point, he believes, and she has no significant action for the rest of the play. However, Tillyard views both *All's Well* and *Measure* as seminal plays leading to Shakespearean romance and its emphasis on forgiveness.

40. Wheeler, Richard P. *Shakespeare's Development and the Problem Comedies: Turn and Counter-Turn.* Berkeley: Univ. of California Press, 1981.
Building on the psychoanalytic analysis of his acknowledged mentor, C. L. Barber, Wheeler examines *All's Well* and *Measure*, written between the festive comedies and the late romances, plays which "share attributes with both groups without quite belonging to either" (1). He devotes a chapter to each play, relating *All's Well* to the festive comedies, the romances, and the sonnets, and *Measure* primarily to the tragedies. Addressing the issue of "the author," Wheeler acknowledges that he is interested in "how the drama presents shifts in relations to deep sources of psychic conflict that can only be explored by assuming the interpenetration of literary form and the evolving temperament of an author" (32). In the problem comedies he locates the central conflicts within young male characters, namely Bertram and Angelo. Bertram he reads as questing for his masculine identity, deeply fearing an oedipal attachment to his mother (or her surrogate Helena) and resistant to the King's often conflicting patriarchal demands. Wheeler contrasts the "ready compliance" of festive heroes like Bassanio and Orlando to Bertram's "recalcitrance" (54). He compares Helena's passion for Bertram to the narrator's passion for the male friend in the sonnets and Helena's cure of the King to Pericles and Leontes's restorations by means of women. As a result of these shared, but generically disparate characteristics, Wheeler says, the play's parts are "mutually antagonistic" (86) and resist resolution. Wheeler reads *Measure*'s Angelo as severely repressed and held in check by the paternal authority of the Duke. Once that is removed, Angelo becomes the victim of his sexual drives. Wheeler also examines Claudio, Isabella, and Vincentio's attitudes toward sexuality. Vincentio distances himself from the

play's struggles, Wheeler argues, by using Angelo as a scapegoat for his own conflicts. For Wheeler this potentially tragic play is "thin[ned] out" (49) toward the end by the controlling, idealized Duke. Wheeler concludes his monograph with a chapter which attempts to trace "trends in Shakespeare's development" (155) through the corpus of his plays so that the reader can see how the problem comedies fit into Wheeler's pattern.

41. Williamson, Marilyn L. *The Patriarchy of Shakespeare's Comedies*, 55–110. Detroit: Wayne State Univ. Press, 1986.

Williamson's book is "a study of power relationships in Shakespeare's comedies" (11) made possible by feminist theory and the work of Michel Foucault. She treats *All's Well* and *Measure* together in a single chapter. Written in the early years of James's reign, these plays present the ruler as parent and thus analyze patriarchal authority in terms of sexuality and the making of marriages. *All's Well* deals with enforced marriages (marriage of court wards, like Bertram, was an issue in James's England) and the use of monarchical power to regulate personal relationships. For Williamson, *Measure* represents the patriarchy's desire to control sexuality, a desire made stronger in England by a sharp increase in population. Because Vincentio has no personal stake in the bed-trick and because he uses his dual identity (as ruler and friar) to wield power which either role alone would not have supported, Williamson finds his representation as patriarchal ruler deeply disturbing, especially as he substitutes himself for Angelo in asking to marry Isabella. Together she believes these two comedies interrogate the state's relationship to its members' sexualities.

42. Yachnin, Paul. "Shakespeare's Problem Plays and the Drama of his Time: *Troilus and Cressida, All's Well That Ends Well, Measure for Measure*." In *A Companion to Shakespeare's Works IV: The Poems, Problem Comedies, Late Plays*, edited by Richard Dutton and Jean E. Howard, 46–68. Oxford: Blackwell Publishing, 2003.

Yachnin views the problem plays as Shakespeare's response to the changing entertainment market of his time. "The 'problem' of the problem plays," he writes, "is only that they are his most radical experiments ... and that they can be understood best against the background of the competitive field of dramatic writing in the decade approximately from 1595 to 1605" (46–47). Shakespeare, he asserts, wrote "populuxe" drama designed to relay "versions of elite culture to socially inclusive audiences" (52). To demonstrate his point, Yachnin chooses a particular feature of each play and considers it in relation to plays being written in the same time frame for Henslowe's company and for the boys' companies. For *Troilus* he examines language and genre in the light of

Chapman's *An Humorous Day's Mirth* and Jonson's *Everyman In His Humour* and *Everyman Out*. In *All's Well*, Yachnin looks at techniques of inward characterization (in comparison to *Hamlet* and to Dekker's *A Shoemaker's Holiday*); and, in *Measure*, he examines political issues (with reference to Heywood's *If You Know Not Me, You Know Nobody* and Middleton's *The Phoenix*). Concluding that Shakespeare's plays are "buzzing with inventiveness" (66), Yachnin suggests they can best be understood in the context of their dramatic competition.

III. TROILUS AND CRESSIDA

A. Editions.

43. Beckerman, Bernard, and Joseph Papp, eds. *Troilus and Cressida. The Festival Shakespeare.* New York: Macmillan, 1967.

This edition memorializes the 1965 production of *Troilus* which Papp directed at the Delacorte Theater in Central Park. The volume contains a history of the play (4–22) by Beckerman, an essay on directing the play by Papp (see no. 112a), eight pages of photographs of the Delacorte production, the text of the play (based on the 1609 Quarto) used in the production and marked to indicate production cuts, some production notes, a brief bibliography, and an appendix which reprints the "Preface to the 1609 Quarto." The most unusual aspect of this edition is Papp's essay on directing the play.

43a. Bevington, David, ed. *Troilus and Cressida.* The Arden Shakespeare, Third Series. London: Thomson Learning, 1998.

Bevington chooses F1 as the "control text" (425) of his edition but adopts readings from both Folio and Quarto texts based on textual grounds, favoring F1 only "in the case of indeterminate claims" (425); "the commitment here is to a text that represents as well as can be done the play's own indeterminate nature" (426). The play's text is copiously annotated and is followed by longer textual notes. Two post-text essays on *Troilus*'s sources and on the play's confused textual history are followed by a comprehensive bibliography. Bevington's introduction is topically organized and includes sections on the play's genre, historical context, thematic issues, and performance history. Bevington's aim is "to present Shakespeare's remarkable and controversial play in something approaching its full complexity" (426). As a result, he uses the introduction not to promote any particular interpretation, but to refer—however briefly—to a great number of critical views of the play.

43b. Dawson, Anthony, ed. *Troilus and Cressida.* The New Cambridge Shakespeare. Cambridge: Cambridge Univ. Press, 2003.

Dawson takes as copy-text the 1609 Quarto, though he discusses the fraught printing history of the play in an extended "Textual Analysis" (234-52) which concludes that the relation between the Quarto and Folio versions "remains uncertain" (250). Both the collation with the Folio and extensive annotations to the text are printed as line notes beneath the text. Dawson's introduction, generously illustrated with production photographs, is arranged by topic and deals with genre, style, date, audiences, relevance to the Earl of Essex, parallel characters, intertextuality, and themes such as value, vision, degree, and "knowing" (35). The introduction concludes with a discussion of the play in performance in each decade from the 1960s to the 1990s. The volume concludes with an appendix on the play's sources and a brief reading list.

44. Hillebrand, Harold N., ed. *Troilus and Cressida: A Variorum Edition.* Philadelphia: J. B. Lippincott, 1953.

Hillebrand prints the First Folio text, but includes significant variant readings from the 1609 Quarto, the three later folios, and selected later editions. These variants are printed on each page immediately below the play's text, and extensive textual notes appear below the variants. Numerous appendices follow the play's text. These treat the printing history, stage history, date and authorship, "*Troilus* and Contemporary Affairs," Ulysses' speech on degree (1.3), the play's sources, staging, Heywood's *Iron Age*, and critical views of the play's individual characters. An extensive bibliography and an index conclude the volume. This edition makes a great deal of information about *Troilus* available and invites readers to draw their own conclusions from that information.

45. Palmer, Kenneth, ed. *Troilus and Cressida.* The Arden Shakespeare, Second Series. London: Routledge, 1982.

Palmer prints an eclectic text with a bias toward Quarto readings. Notes on variant readings are printed on each page below the play's text, and extensive explanatory notes appear below the textual variants. Palmer is especially attentive to cross-referencing verbal patterns and allusions to other Shakespeare plays. The introduction (1-93) discusses the relationship between Quarto and Folio, the play's date, sources, and the play's thematic concerns, with special attention to the role of Time in *Troilus*. Palmer emphasizes the complexity and openness of the play rather than offering many personal interpretive judgments. Five appendices follow the play's text: a discussion of the irregularities in the printing of sheet F of the Quarto; an evaluation of Alexander's theory (see no. 48) that *Troilus* was written for performance at the Inns of Court; a discussion of how passages of Aristotle's *Ethics* inform the play; comments on the source of Ulysses' speech on degree (1.3); and reprinted selections from the play's sources.

46. Taylor, Gary, ed. "Troilus and Cressida." In *William Shakespeare: The Complete Works,* edited by Stanley Wells and Gary Taylor, 807–45. The Oxford Shakespeare. Oxford: Clarendon Press, 1986.

There are two versions of this edition available, one with modernized spelling and another with "original-spelling edition" added to its title page. The original-spelling version follows the 1609 Quarto in printing accidentals and includes an essay by Vivian Salmon on Shakespeare's spelling and punctuation. Otherwise the two versions are the same down to identical pagination of *Troilus*. Following the general principle of the edition to print the "more theatrical text," Taylor prints from the Folio text (see no. 53 for his rationale). A one-page introduction is the only apparatus provided in either version. No textual notes or variants are included except for two Quarto passages omitted from the Folio which Taylor prints as "Additional Passages" at the play's conclusion. An accompanying volume prepared by the same editorial team (*William Shakespeare: A Textual Companion*, 424–43. Oxford: Clarendon Press, 1987) provides an explanation of the choice of copy text, textual notes, rejected Quarto variants, and stage directions from both Quarto and Folio.

47. Walker, Alice, ed. *Troilus and Cressida.* The Cambridge Shakespeare. Cambridge: Cambridge Univ. Press, 1957; pb. 1969.

Walker presents an eclectic text, choosing readings without consistent preference from both the Quarto and Folio texts, which in the case of *Troilus* vary in a number of rather minor ways. Walker's endnotes primarily record variant readings and only occasionally offer textual explanations. A discussion of differences between the Folio and Quarto texts follows the play. A glossary concludes the volume. The introductory materials (ix–xlvi)—dealing with genre, source, circumstances surrounding the first printing and production, characters, and the play's structure—are succinct, though Walker clearly has strong interpretive views of the play. She accepts Cressida as the "drab" described in Henryson's *Testament*, for example, and emphasizes the play's comedy, finding it verging on the mock-heroic. A stage history (xlvii–lvi) written by C. B. Young follows Walker's introduction.

See also no. 28.

B. Dating and Textual Studies.

48. Alexander, Peter. "Troilus and Cressida, 1609." *The Library*, Fourth Series, 9 (1928-9): 267-86.

Alexander deals with the textual transmission of *Troilus*, beginning with the two title pages of the 1609 Quarto. He then discusses the odd placement of *Troilus* in the First Folio (between the Histories and Tragedies, without pagination or an entry in the table of contents). Most of the essay is devoted to discussion of which texts were used by the Folio editors. Alexander's offhand suggestion that Shakespeare "may have written the play for some festivity at one of the Inns of Court" (278) has been made much of by later critics (see nos. 45 and 53). Alexander concludes that the Folio text was based on the 1609 Quarto corrected from a manuscript and that the Quarto gave a later version of the play than did the manuscript by which it was corrected.

49. Greg, W. W. "The Printing of Shakespeare's *Troilus and Cressida* in the First Folio." *The Papers of the Bibliographical Society of America* 45 (1951): 273-82.

Greg engages the question of why *Troilus* was originally withdrawn (after two leaves were printed) from its assigned place following *Romeo and Juliet* in the 1623 Folio and later inserted between the Histories and the Tragedies. Noting the discovery that the original leaves are set from the 1609 Quarto alone, Greg conjectures that, because the rest of the Folio text shows evidence of being corrected from a manuscript, it is likely that the printer of the Quarto refused to allow his copy to be used by Heminge and Condell. Only when a manuscript copy of the play (containing new readings) was found, Greg suggests, could the printing of *Troilus* proceed, using the first-printed leaves but correcting the remaining text by the newly-discovered manuscript.

50. Honigmann, E. A. J. "The Date and Revision of *Troilus and Cressida*." In *Textual Criticism and Literary Interpretation*, edited by Jerome J. McGann, 38-54. Chicago: Univ. of Chicago Press, 1985.

Honigmann revisits the issues of *Troilus*'s date, early stage history, genre, ending, and alternate textual readings. Arguing that the play was written in 1601 at the time of the Essex crisis, he suggests a "try-out" performance, probably at Cambridge, after which the play remained unperformed because of its similarities to some of the aspects of the Essex affair. Honigmann believes Shakespeare intended the play as a tragedy but altered the ending, keeping Troilus alive, to allow for a sequel. He suggests that Shakespeare made a fair copy of the play, altering minor details, for a patron who wished to read it, and continued to emend his foul papers as his company prepared for production. Arguing directly against Taylor's hypothesis (see no. 53), Honigmann sees Shakespeare's fair copy as the basis for the 1609 Quarto and thinks his foul papers, retained by the theater company, are the manuscript by which the Folio corrects the Quarto.

51. **Honigmann, E. A. J.** *Myriad-minded Shakespeare: Essays, Chiefly on the Tragedies and Problem Comedies*, 112-29. New York: St. Martin's Press, 1989.

In his chapter on *Troilus*, Honigmann first lists the problems associated with the play: its date, the canceled title page of the 1609 Quarto, the uncertainty about its early performance history, and its genre. He then proposes the following scenario as a solution to these problems: the play was written in 1601 and was dangerously similar to aspects of the Essex situation; not performed, the play was privately circulated in manuscript and arrived at a printer in 1609, when protests from the King's Men forced a new title page with their name removed. Its genre, Honigmann suggests, was first to be a tragedy but, thinking perhaps of a sequel in which Troilus would be more a warrior than a lover, Shakespeare kept him alive.

52. **Jensen, Phebe.** "The Textual Politics of *Troilus and Cressida*." *Shakespeare Quarterly* 26 (1995): 414-23.

Jensen re-examines Taylor's arguments (see no. 53), taking issue with his decision to omit the epilogue spoken by Pandarus (printed by Taylor as an "Additional Passage"). By this change, Jensen argues, Taylor erases the generic instability of *Troilus* by portraying the play, without real evidence, as first having been presented as a cynical comedy staged for the Inns of Court (a comedy which ended with Pandarus's cynical epilogue) and then (having been revised for a staging at The Globe) as a tragedy which closes with Troilus's speech on the battlefield. Jensen points out the speculative nature of many of Taylor's arguments in order to make the larger point that "textual conclusions are inevitably interpretive" (423) and that editors should avoid whenever possible changes, especially amputations of text, which are not based on strong bibliographic evidence.

53. **Taylor, Gary.** "*Troilus and Cressida*: Bibliography, Performance, and Interpretation." *Shakespeare Studies* 15 (1982): 99-136.

In opposition to other bibliographic scholars (most notably Walker [no. 47] and Greg [no. 49]), Taylor argues that the Quarto is based on Shakespeare's foul papers and that the Folio derives from the Quarto, which had been annotated from a fair copy by Shakespeare, and which was in turn copied by a scribe and became the company promptbook, probably for an Inns of Court performance. As part of his argument supporting the 1609 Quarto as printed from foul papers, Taylor suggests that the puzzling 1609 epistle was really written in 1603 and included among the foul papers. Discovered late in the printing of the Quarto, Taylor theorizes, it caused the printer to alter the preliminaries of the Quarto. Having educed this textual genealogy, Taylor concludes that for accidentals editors should choose Quarto readings, but that for substantive variants the Folio is more authoritative.

See also nos. 28, 43a, 43b, 44, 45, 47.

C. Influences; Sources; Historical and Intellectual Backgrounds; Topicality.

54. Bednarz, James P. "Shakespeare's Purge of Jonson: The Literary Context of *Troilus and Cressida*." *Shakespeare Studies* 21 (1993): 175–212.

Working from a speech in *Return from Parnassus* which claims "our fellow *Shakespeare* hath give [Ben Jonson] a pill that made him beray his credit" (176), Bednarz suggests that *Troilus* is the pill. After background discussion of the Poets' War, Bednarz argues that Jonson is satirized as the braggart soldier Ajax. Shakespeare alerts his audience to the secondary contextual polemics in his play, Bednarz says, by having his prologue "armed," an echo of the "armed prologue" of *Poetaster*. Bednarz cites the quarrel between Ajax and Thersites as a reference to the literary war between Jonson and Marston. *Troilus*, which he reads as Shakespeare's contribution to the Poets' War, demonstrates how the satiric impulse has turned against itself "in a self-subverting struggle for poetic mastery" (206).

55. Clarke, Larry R. "'Mars his heart inflam'd with Venus': Ideology and Eros in Shakespeare's *Troilus and Cressida*." *Modern Language Quarterly* 50 (1989): 209–26.

Clarke argues that *Troilus* is, on one level, a cautionary tale for the English aristocracy. Citing resemblances between the hierarchized and voluptuous Trojans and the court-focused English aristocracy of the late 1590s, Clarke identifies the disorganized but individually powerful Greeks with the Elizabethan "new men" who sought to rise by wealth. Finding in the Greeks both confusion and a sense of social inferiority, Clarke points out that they are nonetheless more successful at survival than the

Trojans, who are weakened by their dependance on an outdated feudal code and by licentiousness and physical self-indulgence.

56. **Cole, Douglas.** "Myth and Anti-Myth: The Case of *Troilus and Cressida*." *Shakespeare Quarterly* 31 (1980): 76–84.

Cole looks at *Troilus* as a play which maintains "a constant and perplexing contrast between idealized conceptions of love and war and their roots in baser and more absurd motivation" (77). He examines Helen, Achilles, Troilus, and particularly Hector as they appear in earlier texts (the myth) and points out how Shakespeare's version both reminds audiences of the myth and simultaneously undercuts it (anti-myth). A necessary component of this anti-myth is that the characters idealize their mistakes and selfish choices as heroic gestures, and thus "the fraudulent quality of human idealism is exposed and mocked" (83).

57. **Donaldson, E. Talbot.** *The Swan at the Well: Shakespeare Reading Chaucer*, 74–118. New Haven: Yale Univ. Press, 1985.

Donaldson believes Shakespeare to have been a sophisticated reader of Chaucer, someone who recognized the multi-faceted and ambiguous nature of Chaucer's work. Donaldson devotes two chapters of his brief monograph to a comparison of *Troilus* with Chaucer's *Troilus and Criseyde*. In the first, he examines Criseyde and Cressida, finding them both ambiguous, two-sided characters who are both good and bad. Chaucer's character, he argues, is often unjustly elevated by critics while Shakespeare's is unjustly denigrated. In the next chapter, he examines the two Troilus characters, arguing that Chaucer's is the more idealistic and more considerate lover while Shakespeare's Troilus is merely self-absorbed.

58. **Freund, Elizabeth.** "'Ariachne's broken woof': The Rhetoric of Citation in *Troilus and Cressida*." In *Shakespeare and the Question of Theory*, edited by Patricia Parker and Geoffrey Hartman, 19–36. New York: Methuen, 1985.

Freund presents *Troilus* as an example of the Renaissance writer's dilemma between reinscribing classical texts and showing originality, arguing that it constantly raises questions of intertextuality, of a Cressida who "is, and is not" (5.2.142). For Freund, the characters are both inscriptions of themselves as seen in earlier texts and mimetic representations that persuade readers of their dramatic life. The essay examines how the play at the same time both accepts and refuses its powerful precursor texts by Homer and Chaucer.

59. **Glasser, Marvin.** "Baroque Formal Elements in Shakespeare's *Troilus and Cressida*." *The Upstart Crow* 6 (1986): 54–70.

Arguing that *Troilus* exemplifies the breakdown of sixteenth-century epistemology, a dislocation mirrored in the visual arts of the period, Glasser discusses the dissolving of temporal and spatial boundaries in *Troilus*. He finds a similar disjunction in the play's characters, many of whom have two distinct identities. The audience's theatrical expectations are mocked, according to Glasser, and its perspective constantly shifts. As a result, he says, characters and events are judged subjectively, not according to a prescribed image or code.

60. **James, Heather.** *Shakespeare's Troy: Drama, Politics, and the Translation of Empire*, 85-118. Cambridge: Cambridge Univ. Press, 1997.

James's monograph investigates how Shakespeare uses the materials of imperial Rome to "legitimate the cultural place of the theater" (1) in early modern England. In her chapter on *Troilus* James examines the use of the Troy legend by Ariosto, Geoffrey of Monmouth, and the Tudor monarchs, concluding "At the time of Shakespeare's play, the lovers and colossal warriors of the Troy legend stood variously prized, devalued, and redeemed" (89). Shakespeare, she claims, staged the divisive ideologies associated with the story, refusing "to privilege or adjudicate among versions of the legend" (89). As support, she examines the doubleness of Troilus, of the play's genre, of Paris and Helen, of Cressida, and of the Greeks in the competing traditions. In conclusion, she asks what motivated Shakespeare to further "contaminate" (113) the Troy story, and discusses the printing of Chapman's Homer and the fall of the Earl of Essex as possible motivations.

61. **Mallin, Eric S.** "Emulous Factions and the Collapse of Chivalry: *Troilus and Cressida*." *Representations* 29 (1990): 145-79.

This new historicist essay argues that the political strategy of pitting one court faction against another in the late Elizabethan court is represented in the Greek camp in *Troilus*. According to this view, Essex finds representation in the narcissistic, self-indulgent Achilles; moreover, the image of Essex has been bifurcated because he is also figured in the falsely chivalric behavior of Hector, who like Essex is destroyed by a rival group. For Mallin, this warped version of chivalry effectively displaces the women—Cressida and Helen—who are nominally the cause of chivalric behavior, much as Elizabeth was displaced in her last years by male negotiations for power.

62. **Mead, Stephen X.** " 'Thou art chang'd': Public Value and Personal Identity in *Troilus and Cressida*." *Journal of Medieval and Renaissance Studies* 22 (1992): 237-59.

Mead looks at *Troilus* in the light of extra-literary debates, current in early modern England, over the meaning of money, wealth, and exchange. Asserting that in *Troilus* money is language and language is money, Mead compares Cressida and Helen, the "wealth" of the play's world, to the "wealth" of England. For Mead, Helen is "a priceless abstract: a signified" (252). At first Cressida shares this pricelessness, he asserts, but her value becomes fixed once Troilus beds her; when Cressida is exchanged, her value is "set down" (254) or debased, as happened to coins in international trade. As Elizabeth and James tried to assert that coins retained their old absolute value, so Troilus wishes Cressida to keep the value he assigned her and, when she does not, Mead argues, Troilus assumes she was counterfeit from the start.

63. **Southall, Raymond.** "*Troilus and Cressida* and the Spirit of Capitalism." In *Shakespeare in a Changing World*, edited by Arnold Kettle, 217-32. London: Lawrence & Wishart, 1964.

Southall's thesis is that the Trojan story of chivalry and courtly love is deliberately coarsened in Shakespeare's play, revealing a new Renaissance ethic which saw all human relationships in terms of commerce. The essay traces the commercial imagery used by Troilus and others in reference both to love and to war, and concludes that the body politic portrayed in the play is sick and dying of over-indulgence. In Southall's view, the play presents capitalism as destroying without hope of redemption.

64. **Spear, Gary.** "Shakespeare's 'Manly' Parts: Masculinity and Effeminacy in *Troilus and Cressida*." *Shakespeare Quarterly* 44 (1993): 409-22.

Examining the concept of effeminacy in early modern culture, Spear suggests that—in contrast to contemporary definitions—it then implied delicacy, love of excessive pleasure (especially pleasure with women), and an anti-heroic military ethos. Thus, for Spear, Achilles and Troilus, both of whom withdraw from battle because of love of a woman, are "effeminate" and must return to the masculine sphere of battle. The essay argues that, in this nexus of gender and power relationships, women are reduced to objects (pearls) as a means of containing their sexuality and effeminating pressures.

65. **Suzuki, Mihoko.** *Metamorphoses of Helen: Authority, Difference and the Epic*, 210-57. Ithaca: Cornell Univ. Press, 1989.

Suzuki's book studies Helen, both as motivating force and as stated goal, in epic retellings of her story. After examining her presence in classical epics and in *The Fairie Queene*, Suzuki concludes her study with discussion of *Troilus*. She begins with Cressida, constantly compared to Helen and, like Helen, figured as merchandise that becomes degraded once men use it. Cressida's subjectivity in the play is compared to Helen's lack of it; Helen, she says, is reduced to a cardboard collection of nouns and adjectives. Suzuki argues that Shakespeare scapegoats Helen in place of Cressida (239). Troilus is unable to see Cressida as one; he conflates her with Helen and later splits her in two. Suzuki suggests that Cressida in *Troilus* is modeled on the Helen of *The Iliad*, a symbol of the doubleness of the war effort, a character initially possessed of subjectivity who abandons it and accepts her stereotyped personification as falsehood.

See also nos. 28, 29, 33, 38, 43a, 43b, 44, 45, 47, 50, 51, 79, 91, 93, 99.

D. Language and Linguistics.

66. Barfoot, C. C. "*Troilus and Cressida*: 'Praise us as we are tasted.'" *Shakespeare Quarterly* 39 (1988): 45–57.

Barfoot revisits the issue of value in *Troilus*, suggesting that neither the valuation nor the state of the valuer remains stable in the play. Examining the difference between advertisement (in part a reliance on past literary reputation) and performance in the "heroes," Barfoot suggests that the characters expect to be valued at their own estimation, to be taken at their word. To undergird his emphasis on value, Barfoot undertakes a detailed examination of the play's words, noting the shared etymology of "praise," "prize," and "price" and how often they substitute for one another in the lines of *Troilus*. Likewise, he discusses "taste" and "test," noting the link between imagery of food and appetite and that of valuation. The play's mercantile imagery, he argues, engenders skepticism in an audience about the ability of literature to tell the truth, to be other than propaganda or salesmanship.

67. Colie, Rosalie L. *Shakespeare's Living Art*, 317–49. Princeton: Princeton Univ. Press, 1974.

Colie's book is concerned with the ways Shakespeare "used, misused, criticized, recreated, and sometimes revolutionized the received topics, and devices, large and small, of his artful craft" (3). Her final chapter considers the empty rhetoric of *Troilus*, where well-established literary heroes are drained of meaning until they become only self-mocking cliches, most dramatically exemplified by the transformation of Troilus, Cressida, and Pandarus into mere figures of speech. In a play filled with meaningless questions, Colie argues, even the traditional forms of heroic drama and romance are interrogated and emptied of meaning: the war is not heroic and the love affair is neither comic nor romantic. For Colie, the play thwarts expectation and jolts its audience out of its ordinary ways of perceiving.

68. Danson, Lawrence. *Tragic Alphabet: Shakespeare's Drama of Language,* 68–96. New Haven: Yale Univ. Press, 1974.

Danson's book deals with linguistic inadequacy as a hallmark of Shakespearean tragedy. In the acting out of death, Danson points out, words fail and silence reigns. In *Troilus,* Danson finds not a tragedy but a parody of tragedy, where all the play's speeches and plans dissolve, not into silence, but into chaos. In *Troilus,* he argues, the arts of language interrogate the efficacy of language in a world without order.

69. Greene, Gayle. "Language and Value in Shakespeare's *Troilus and Cressida.*" *Studies in English Literature 1500–1900* 21 (1981): 271–85.

Greene argues that *Troilus* demonstrates the dissolution of language as a way of examining the breakdown of social and moral order. Noting that the seventeenth century was skeptical about language and its relation to reality, an attitude which differed markedly from the similitudes and theory of correspondences found in the sixteenth century, Greene sees *Troilus* as mediating the change by suggesting the difficulty of speaking truth, by using language that is stiffly rhetorical, and by twisting language. Words do not correspond to deeds in *Troilus,* Greene continues, and character evaluations in one scene are contradicted in the next. The play's interest in comparisons, vows, and tautologies all point, for Greene, to a recognition of the emptiness and futility of words.

70. Hillman, David. "The Gastric Epic: *Troilus and Cressida.*" *Shakespeare Quarterly* 48 (1997): 295–313.

Asserting that "the relation between language and the body out of which it emanates" (296) lies at the heart of *Troilus,* Hillman sees the play as restoring the words of overtextualized characters to the bodies which produced them. Hillman cites Nietzsche's concern with entrails (as a way to reveal the reality beneath rhetoric) as an analogue to the play's preoccupation with high rhetoric undercut by images of bloated entrails. The play's perverse and insatiable appetites reduce all desire to a desire for food, Hillman argues, and to a cannibalism which makes repulsive the play's overblown language. Only Antenor, the character for whom Cressida is exchanged, offers an alternative "to the surfeit of degraded language with which he is surrounded" (313), says Hillman, by remaining completely mute.

See also nos. 42, 62, 78, 83, 85, 91, 93, 99.

E. Criticism.

71. Adams, Howard C. " 'What Cressid Is.' " In *Sexuality and Politics in Renaissance Drama*, edited by Carole Levin and Karen Robertson, 75–93. Studies in Renaissance Literature 10. Lewiston, NY: Mellen, 1991.

Adams attempts to articulate what Cressida is by a detailed examination of her speeches and interactions with Troilus. He argues that she is originally of two minds: to use her beauty to advantage to attract male protectors and to commit to a faithful relationship with Troilus. Troilus's words, Adams believes, convince Cressida to commit to him, but his morning-after responses, including his nervousness about her fidelity, unsettle her, and with Diomedes she returns to the same uncertainty she originally felt. Adams asserts that the world of the play denies Cressida the stability she needs for "satisfactory self-fashioning" (89).

72. Adelman, Janet. *Suffocating Mothers: Fantasies of Maternal Origin in Shakespeare's Plays, "Hamlet" to "The Tempest,"* 38–75. New York: Routledge, 1992.

Adelman's book examines "masculinity and the maternal body" (2). Her psychological reading of *Troilus* argues that Troilus's passion for Cressida is infantilized and largely oral. Troilus unwittingly expects to be satiated by her once their union is consummated. The consummation soils Cressida as a maternal object in Troilus's eyes, making necessary his separation from her when she is traded to the Greeks. This separation, according to Adelman, triggers Troilus's emergence into full manhood as he returns to the battlefield.

73. Adelman, Janet. " 'This Is and Is Not Cressid': The Characterization of Cressida." In *The (M)other Tongue: Essays in Feminist Psychoanalytic Interpretation*, edited by Shirley Nelson Garner, Claire Kahane, and Madelon Sprengnether, 119–41. Ithaca: Cornell Univ. Press, 1985.

Adelman sees Cressida as a "whole character" (121) in the early acts of *Troilus*; witty, she reveals herself in soliloquy and projects vulnerability. Once she goes to the Greeks, Adelman argues, Cressida retreats into opacity: her motivations are no longer accessible; instead the audience sees her as Troilus does, and Troilus's desire, according to this essay, is associated with longing for union with a maternal figure. Cressida's betrayal and their earlier sexual union, Adelman continues, "soil" the mother for Troilus; Cressida's betrayal allows him to separate her sexual from her ideal maternal self, making it her infidelity rather than his sexuality which soils. Thus, Adelman believes that Cressida's internal psychological consistency is sacrificed because of Troilus's infantilized fantasy of the mother.

74. Bayley, John. "Time and the Trojans." *Essays in Criticism* 25 (1975): 55–73.

Bayley claims that *Troilus* is unlike other Shakespeare plays in its evocation of time. That is, he believes its characters live only in the present. The audience cannot envision for them, nor do the characters seem to recognize for themselves, a past and a future. The play seems to deny that the legendary war and its warriors ever existed as time reported them, according to Bayley. Unlike Shakespeare's other railers, he points out, Thersites receives no punishment or setback, perhaps because there is no way within the play world to rebut his assertions that all is lechery. Bayley finds no significant difference between the Greeks and the Trojans. He concludes that the curious flatness of the characters is the result of the dramatist's working within the dramatic present; by so doing he relinquishes any external vantage point from which to view his characters.

75. Berger, Harry Jr. "*Troilus and Cressida*: The Observer as Basilisk." *Comparative Drama* 2 (1968): 122–36.

Berger begins by commenting on the Chorus of *Henry V*, noting that it both brings into parallel and contrasts history and drama, projecting the ceremony of history into the theatrical experience. By contrast, he thinks the prologue to *Troilus* is cynical and unconcerned, providing no interpretive framework for the audience. Similarly, Berger provides a skeptical reading of Ulysses' speech on order (1.3), claiming it is a rhetorical stopgap in which degree becomes a matter of perspective. Berger then examines the perspective of Thersites, observer and interpreter of the play's action. The audience struggles, he believes, with whether to interpret Thersites' railing as jaundiced envy or legitimate commentary. The play becomes, in Berger's view, an examination of perspective, a staging of an old order in the light of contemporary viewpoints, subjecting traditional views of order to theatrical experiment.

76. Bernhardt. W. W. "Shakespeare's *Troilus and Cressida* and Dryden's *Truth Found Too Late*." *Shakespeare Quarterly* 20 (1969): 129–41.

Bernhardt looks at the changes Dryden made (see no. 117) in Shakespeare's *Troilus*—simplifying ornate diction; reworking the plot to give it the form of an heroic tragedy; "finishing" Shakespeare's characters by ennobling the potentially heroic (Troilus) and turning the potentially comic (Pandarus and Thersites) into mere clowns. Though he argues that Dryden had seen something important at the heart of Shakespeare's play—a focus on Troilus—Bernhardt defends Shakespeare on each point Dryden changed. He asserts that the play deals with a potentially heroic figure whose language and actions betray his inexperience and that *Troilus* is a kind of *bildungsroman*.

77. Brooks, Harold. "*Troilus and Cressida*: Its Dramatic Unity and Genre." In *"Fanned and Winnowed Opinions": Shakespearean Essays presented to Harold Jenkins*, edited by John W. Mahon and Thomas A. Pendleton, 6–25. London: Methuen, 1987.

Brooks asserts the unity of *Troilus* by enumerating the parallels between the love plot and the war plot: Troilus is a romantic idealist balanced by Diomed, a cynical seducer; Hector's devotion to honor is balanced by Achilles' opportunism, and so on. He concludes that the play's genre is also a balance: *Troilus* is both romantic tragedy and bitter comedy.

78. Burns, M. M. "*Troilus and Cressida*: The Worst of Both Worlds." *Shakespeare Studies* 13 (1980): 105–30.

Burns's thesis is that *Troilus*, set in a world at war, presents a disintegrated image of humanity. Noting that the play's language about women is consistently ugly, Burns suggests that frustration over the war is displaced onto a woman, Helen, who is seen as object or image, never as an individual. For him, the play portrays parallel manipulations of women and soldiers: Cressida and Hector, for example, both go to the Greeks where they are "carved up" (126) verbally, as Hector later will be literally. Burns says that the play subjects both men and women to pressures that destroy their humanity.

79. Campbell, Oscar James. *Comicall Satyre and Shakespeare's "Troilus and Cressida,"* 185–234. Los Angeles: Adcraft Press, 1938.

Campbell's thesis is that when prose and poetic satires were banned in England in 1599, dramatists such as Jonson and Marston promptly adapted their tone and matter to the stage, producing what Campbell terms "comicall satyres." Formed from a "synthesis of the practice of the ancients in old comedy and the theories of the Renaissance based on classical precept and example" (14), this new dramatic genre flourished, according to Campbell, in the period from 1599 to 1603. Shakespeare's sole contribution to this fashionable new genre, he argues, is *Troilus*. In both the war and the love plots all rational control is abandoned. In the love plot, Shakespeare exhibits two young sensualists whose licentiousness is exposed. Campbell argues against finding topical satire—Ben Jonson (whom some critics see figured in Ajax) or Essex (Achilles)—in *Troilus*, but suggests that the play displays the more general satiric themes of disillusionment and cynicism. This dominant tone explains for Campbell the play's lack of traditional closure.

80. **Charnes, Linda.** *Notorious Identity: Materializing the Subject in Shakespeare*, 70–102. Cambridge: Harvard Univ. Press, 1993.

Charnes's monograph studies Shakespearean plays containing figures who were already "notorious" in Shakespeare's day and what happens when those figures are "reiterated" in Shakespeare's text. Explaining that she intends to praise *Troilus* for its deformity, which is the source of its power, Charnes reminds the reader that the characters of this play are fixed by their previous representations. In Charnes's psychoanalytic approach, Shakespeare's characters deny foreknowledge of their own actions in language that constantly reminds the audience of their predetermined fate. She argues that the mimetic presence of stage action subverts the "authorized" textual representation of character. She also examines the tension between the "desire for presence" (98), for what is seen on stage, and the translation of bodies into texts to be consumed by an audience that already knows the story. Charnes deals with the ways in which *Troilus* responds to its status as a text with pre-determined, pre-scripted characters.

81. **Dodd, Mark Robert.** "The History of *Troilus and Cressida*." *The Upstart Crow* 11 (1991): 39–51.

This essay argues that *Troilus* is a history play, a portrait of a doomed pagan world. To support his thesis, Dodd isolates in *Troilus* features of a history play: episodic structure, an historical theme, and emphasis on plot manipulation at the expense of consistency of character. As a Shakespearean history play, *Troilus* is unusual, Dodd asserts, only in the origins of its subject in non-Christian, non-English history.

82. **Dollimore, Jonathan.** *Radical Tragedy: Religion, Ideology and Power in the Drama of Shakespeare and his Contemporaries*, 40–50. Chicago: Univ. of Chicago Press, 1984.

Dollimore's study focuses on the "subversive preoccupations" of Jacobean drama, namely its undermining of religious orthodoxy, critique of ideology, "demystification of political and power relations," and "decentering of 'man'" (4). Comparing *Troilus* to Marston's *Antonio* plays, Dollimore claims that Troilus, rather than being destroyed by grief, is brutalized by Cressida's betrayal. He sees the two philosophical debates in the play—on order and on value—undercut by the play's action; even time is a surrogate universal, called on by characters to legitimate fatalism. For Dollimore, the play is marked by disjunctions and thus is like other Jacobean tragedies. He suggests that Troilus internalizes rather than transcends the violence of his society. The chapter concludes that the play's political, social, and ideological contradictions lead to a subversion of the ideals of Christian humanism.

83. **Dusinberre, Juliet.** " 'Troilus and Cressida' and the Definition of Beauty." *Shakespeare Survey* 36 (1983): 85-95.

Dusinberre declares that the problem of how to define beauty is central to *Troilus*, and that beauty is embodied in the play by beautiful women, Helen and Cressida. Comparing the play's interrogation of beauty to that found in Plato's *Hippias*, Dusinberre notes that beauty is judged comparatively (Cressida compared to Helen), by cost (is Helen worth the war?), and by the senses, never as inner beauty. According to her, *Troilus* dramatizes the inseparability of the foul and fair in human experience, as well as the disintegration of language as it tries to encompass the paradox. Her study emphasizes the sterility of this play, where pursuit of beauty leads not to procreation but to disease and war.

84. **Eagleton, Terence.** *Shakespeare and Society: Critical Studies in Shakespearean Drama*, 13-38. New York: Schocken Books, 1967.

Eagleton's book explores the tension in several Shakespeare plays between the self as individual and the self as responsible to, and part of, society. In *Troilus*, he sees this tension crystallizing as a struggle between individual spontaneity, which recognizes no fixed values or principles, and social responsibility, grounded in reason and a shared value system. Eagleton argues that both the Greeks and Trojans, in different ways, attempt to fuse reason with spontaneity, and individualism with social responsibility, and concludes that both fail.

85. **Empson, William.** *Some Versions of Pastoral*, 32-41. New York: New Directions, 1960.

Empson's much-cited remarks on the double plot in *Troilus* point to the structure as setting up a mutual comparison that illuminates both plots. For Empson, Cressida's situation must be taken as seriously as the war because it occupies an equal position in the play; ironically, the audience sees her as more important than she sees herself. Empson locates much of the play's energy in its language, especially in its subdued puns, and demonstrates his point by examining the double uses of the word "general" as it appears in the play.

86. **Fly, Richard D.** " 'Suited in Like Conditions as our Argument': Imitative Form in Shakespeare's *Troilus and Cressida*." *Studies in English Literature 1500-1900* 15 (1975): 273-92.

In this formalist essay which argues that form echoes content in *Troilus*, Fly opens with a brief survey of earlier critics of the play's structure. Fly continues by pointing out a series of disjunctions, anti-climaxes, and irrelevancies in the play's chain of events and characterizations. Noting repeated processions which end with minor or worthless characters, Fly relates them to rhetorical catalogs which move toward diminishment. Fly's conclusion is that the play's form and its vision manifest chaos, serving as a microcosmic view of the uncertainties of Jacobean society.

87. **Girard, René.** "The Politics of Desire in *Troilus and Cressida.*" In *Shakespeare and the Question of Theory*, edited by Patricia Parker and Geoffrey Hartman, 188-209. New York: Methuen, 1985.

Girard argues that *Troilus* focuses on mimetic desire which he says takes two forms: desire which is intensified by the presence of a rival desire (which it imitates) and desire heightened by the unexpected withholding of love or admiration. He finds such mimetic desire in both the love plot (Troilus's desire for Cressida, heightened first by her withholding love and then by her transfer to Diomedes) and in the war plot (Ulysses manipulates Achilles by creating Ajax as his rival and by withholding attention from Achilles). Lechery and war are the same, he claims, and are triggered by similar manipulative strategies. For Girard, such a reading explains the prominence of Pandarus and Ulysses, the two master manipulators of desire.

88. **Greene, Gayle.** "Shakespeare's Cressida: 'A Kind of Self.'" In *The Woman's Part: Feminist Criticism of Shakespeare*, edited by Carolyn Lenz, Gayle Greene, and Carol Neely, 133-49. Urbana: Univ. of Illinois Press, 1980.

Noting that human nature is shaped by social forces and values, Greene argues that Cressida is the sum of male opinions. For Greene, Cressida becomes what men believe her to be—merchandise whose worth is diminished as she travels from hand to hand. Cressida, in this reading, is aware of herself as commodity and tries to market herself to advantage, faltering briefly when her emotional attachment to Troilus strengthens. As an astute but helpless commentator, she watches her own destruction, Greene argues. Unlike Shakespeare's other plays, according to Greene, *Troilus* shows its young lovers to be tainted and shaped by the corrupt society in which they live.

89. **Greenfield, Matthew A.** "Fragments of Nationalism in *Troilus and Cressida.*" *Shakespeare Quarterly* 51 (2000): 181-200.

Greenfield argues that, unlike Shakespeare's history plays where the nation ultimately heals and community is restored, *Troilus* reveals the "nation as a collection of fictions" (181). As evidence, Greenfield points to the play's failure to mention the national myth of the Trojan origins of Britain and to the satire of Achilles and Ulysses which leaves no value intact. For Greenfield, Thersites is primarily responsible for discounting nationalism as he indiscriminately cheers both sides into battle and details the bastards, cuckolds, traitors, and racial hybrids who populate the play. Greenfield traces a pattern of characters pulled away from their communities who go on to destabilize relatives, friends, or lovers. Calchas, the Trojan traitor, pulls his daughter from the Trojan to the Greek camp. This destabilization not only fragments national identities, according to Greenfield, but also leads to splits within individual characters: Cressida and Hector are his chief examples. Greenfield concludes by comparing portraits of Hector in Heywood's *The Iron Age* and Dryden's revision of *Troilus* (see no. 117) with Shakespeare's Hector. In the other texts, Hector is unambiguously heroic in support of a nationalist ideology, which Greenfield believes is called into question by Shakespeare's play.

90. **Harris, Sharon M.** "Feminism and Shakespeare's Cressida: '*If* I be false . . .'" *Women's Studies* 18 (1990): 65-82.

This essay surveys criticism of *Troilus* from the late 1940s to the mid-1980s for its attitudes towards Cressida. Harris finds six major patterns into which responses fall: virtual silence; distinguishing Cressida simply as "whore" (the most pervasive response); seeing her as inherently limited and thus bound to betray Troilus; reading her as part of a literary convention that dictates her behavior; equating women with disorder in society and therefore seeing Cressida as disruptive of social order; claiming that Cressida does the only thing she can, considering her circumstances and environment. Harris then briefly considers feminist responses to each pattern and suggests avenues that feminist scholars might pursue in the study of *Troilus*. Her "Works Cited" provides an extensive bibliography of twentieth-century criticism of the play.

91. **Hyland, Peter.** "Legitimacy in Interpretation: The Bastard Voice in *Troilus and Cressida*." *Mosaic* 26 (1993): 1-13.

Hyland focuses on Thersites, whose voice he believes represents all who are excluded from the play's social hierarchy. Despite Thersites' marginalization by the play's characters and by critics, Hyland argues that he is truly subversive and cannot be neutralized by theories of containment. Isolating Thersites' brief encounter with the Greek bastard Margarelon (5.5), Hyland suggests that this otherwise purposeless passage calls attention to bastardy and proclaims Thersites "spokesman for a whole constituency of those who have been marginalized and disaffected by the tyranny of 'legitimate' power" (6). Exploring the place of bastardy in early modern culture, Hyland concludes that the bastard "was the quintessential victim" (8). He opposes Thersites to Ulysses, spokesman for the "legitimate." Thersites' obscenities distance him as much as possible from Ulysses' authoritative voice, parodying in a Bakhtinian carnivalesque voice the order Ulysses describes. Thersites' only power, Hyland concludes, is his words, and to ignore them is to ignore the dispossessed of the world.

92. **Kaufmann, A. J.** "Ceremonies for Chaos: The Status of *Troilus and Cressida*." *ELH* 32 (1965): 139–59.

Kaufmann reads *Troilus* as a recapitulation of the principal thematic concerns in Shakespeare's plays of the late 1590s and as a prolegomenon to the mature tragedies. For Kaufmann, the play's multiple perspectives (most clearly exemplified in the scene where Troilus watches Cressida and Diomedes), and lack of a secure vantage point for judgment, make it only a forerunner of tragedy. The play's dominant theme, in his view, is self-consumption of the very values it seems initially to set forth.

93. **Kimbrough, Robert.** *Shakespeare's "Troilus and Cressida" and its Setting.* Cambridge: Harvard Univ. Press, 1964.

Kimbrough describes the methodology of his study of *Troilus* as "measuring puzzling aspects of a given play against its sources" (viii) and against analogous aspects of contemporary plays. After chapters dealing with the play's theatrical context, its relation to its sources, and its plot structure, Kimbrough devotes the remainder of his study to aspects of plot and to the play's rhetoric. After discussing it within the context of a number of Tudor–Stuart plays, including others by Shakespeare, Kimbrough concludes that the play is a theatrical failure but not an artistic one. He believes that *Troilus* is a curious mixture of old and new, not quite fitting the demands of either the public or the private theater.

94. **Kott, Jan.** *Shakespeare our Contemporary.* Trans. Boleslaw Taborski, 75–83. New York: Doubleday, 1966.

As its title suggests, Kott's monograph focuses on reading Shakespeare's plays in relation to their significance for the contemporary world. In his brief remarks on *Troilus*, Kott stresses the *"buffo"* tone (75), broadly played in the Greek camp, more subtle among the Trojans. He characterizes the play as "a dispute about the existence of a moral order in a cruel and irrational world" (77). Labelling the Greeks as practical tradesmen and the Trojans as anachronistic absolutists, Kott focuses on young Cressida, raised in wartime and caught between the two sides.

95. **Labranche, Linda.** "Visual Patterns and Linking Analogues in *Troilus and Cressida*." *Shakespeare Quarterly* 37 (1986): 440–50.

Labranche focuses on visual "language" in *Troilus*, patterns made obvious in staged productions. Among these she includes the repeated "handing-over" of Cressida, the "many against one" motif which culminates in the slaughter of Hector, the repeated examples of unsoldierly soldiers and friendly enemies. Examining the webs of association, both visual and verbal, among characters, she argues that such associations make an audience's evaluation of characters more difficult and complex, and thus challenge the legends behind those characters, stereotypes such as "true as Troilus."

96. Lynch, Stephen J. "Hector and the Theme of Honor in *Troilus and Cressida*." *The Upstart Crow* 7 (1987): 68–79.

Lynch argues that Hector, seen by some critics as an exception to the play's decadence, is a contradictory character more concerned with public reputation than with intrinsic value. Despite his noble qualities, Hector is not introspective, Lynch maintains, and never recognizes the gap between genuine honor and the superficial, public honor he pursues. Lynch says that while Hector remains an ideal hero to the Trojans and Greeks, he typifies, for the audience, the failure of Greek and Trojan society.

97. Lynch, Stephen J. "The Idealism of Shakespeare's Troilus." *South Atlantic Review* 51 (1986): 19–29.

Lynch finds the character of Troilus idealistic, enmeshed in self-love, and lacking in self-knowledge. He believes that Troilus fails to see Cressida as she is, seeing instead a female version of himself. Though Troilus promises much, Lynch finds that Troilus delivers little. He contrasts him to the humbler Troilus of Chaucer. Though Lynch admits sympathy for Troilus in the betrayal scene, he finds no evidence of growth or self-awareness in Troilus by the play's end.

98. Lynch, Stephen J. "Shakespeare's Cressida: 'A Woman of Quick Sense.'" *Philological Quarterly* 63 (1984): 357–68.

Arguing that "quick sense" (4.5.54) means quick wit as well as ready sensuality, Lynch focuses on Cressida's intelligence and understanding of the situations in which she finds herself. He sees her as introspective and self-aware, acting first as critic of the Trojan heroes and love, and later as critic of her own behavior. Lynch believes that Cressida behaves as is expected of her by the social group in which she finds herself. Thus, Troilus briefly influences her to adopt his idealism, Lynch says, but she returns to witty cynicism when she is transferred to the Greeks (who read her as "whore") to whose expectations she ruefully conforms, even as she points out her own weakness and foretells her future.

99. **Norbrook, David.** "Rhetoric, Ideology, and the Elizabethan World Picture." In *Renaissance Rhetoric*, edited by Peter Mack, 140-64. New York: St. Martin's Press, 1994.

In an essay which resists sharp binary opposition between Renaissance rhetoric and ideology, Norbrook argues that rhetoric was a critical political force in the early modern period, that it promoted debates about political legitimacy. To demonstrate, he analyzes the rhetorical strategies of texts Tillyard used in *The Elizabethan World Picture*, one of which is Ulysses' speech on degree (1.3) from *Troilus*. His conclusion about the speech is that Ulysses is both parodying Patroclus' parody of the Greek leaders in order to alert the Greeks to their egotism, and trying to persuade them to act for the common good.

100. **Novy, Marianne L.** *Love's Argument: Gender Relations in Shakespeare*, 110-24. Chapel Hill: Univ. of North Carolina Press, 1984.

Novy's book examines two conflicts present in Shakespeare's plays, "between mutuality and patriarchy" and between "emotion and control" (3). Both, she asserts, involve the politics of gender. Novy pairs *Troilus* with *Romeo and Juliet* in a single chapter because she sees both as portraying relationships between young lovers in which women have relative equality as long as the relationship is private. In Novy's view, these private worlds are threatened in both plays by violence. Whereas Novy sees Romeo and Juliet building a verbal rapport and a love, she finds Cressida and Troilus to be peculiarly self-centered, unable to find verbal rapport. Their relationship, she argues, is one of "unintegrated sexuality" (115) or lust. She believes that their private world echoes their larger world, in which gender relations are skewed by the treatment of women as property.

101. **O'Rourke, James.** "'Rule in Unity' and Otherwise: Love and Sex in *Troilus and Cressida*." *Shakespeare Quarterly* 43 (1992): 139-58.

This Lacanian psychoanalytical reading focuses on the relationship between Troilus and Cressida, with some observations also about Thersites and Patroclus, whom O'Rourke parallels with Cressida as slaves in a master-slave dialectic. O'Rourke argues that "The Law of the Father" or patriarchy is responsible for the corruption of sexuality in the play. He examines the different bases of the lovers' vows of mutuality: Troilus believes he will win fame—recognition within Lacan's Symbolic Order—for his fidelity, while Cressida knows that her place in the Order will be as a "thing" that enables Troilus to find satisfaction. O'Rourke explains that Cressida's defection destroys Troilus's belief in natural order and that the total breakdown of Symbolic Order is imaged in the play's final moments by Pandarus's diseased body.

102. Rabkin, Norman. *Shakespeare and the Common Understanding*, 31–60. New York: The Free Press, 1967.

Rabkin's study focuses on a mode of vision which sees the world in terms of opposites, each equally valid, so that to choose between them is impossible. This vision of constant, irresolvable tension, Rabkin calls "complementarity." Arguing that complementarity is characteristic of Shakespeare's drama, Rabkin goes on to examine a number of his plays. He sees *Troilus* as a brilliant example of the use of a double plot to convey a complex theme, a vision of complementarity. Reading the play as intricately patterned and unified, Rabkin asserts that the central theme is the relation of time to value, that value is always a function of time. Rabkin concludes his remarks on complementarity by pairing *Troilus* with *Othello* as his best example of "the complementary nature of [Shakespeare's] vision" (58), seeing both plays set in worlds where time determines "events over which the actors themselves do not have final control" (60).

103. Slights, Camille. "The Parallel Structure of *Troilus and Cressida*." *Shakespeare Quarterly* 25 (1974): 42–51.

Slights argues that the shape of *Troilus*—its parallel characters, scenes, and ideas—defines both its meaning and its tone. Changing O. J. Campbell's description of the play as "comical satire" (no. 79) to tragic satire, Slights examines a number of parallel scenes, arguing that they set up a pattern of recall and expectation in the audience. The technique of parallelism, she believes, allows Shakespeare to shape audience members' reactions, to prevent them from responding with either sentimentality or cynicism, and instead to help them understand the play's vision of absurdity and frustration.

104. Stein, Arnold. "*Troilus and Cressida*: The Disjunctive Imagination." *ELH* 36 (1969): 145–67.

Commenting that the dramatic experience derived from *Troilus* is "a nightmare we have got used to" (145), Stein discusses a number of individual passages and characters that reveal inconsistency, disproportion, mis-emphasis, anti-climax, and the often-noted gap between the play's rhetoric and action. Stein's most extended analysis is of the scene between Cressida and Diomedes witnessed by three eavesdroppers (5.2). Calling *Troilus* a play that "fails as tragedy" (164), Stein concludes that it forces the audience to witness a society in dissolution by emphasizing interruptions, break-downs, gaps, and absences. He characterizes the play as an exercise of the dramatic imagination in revolt against itself.

105. Traub, Valerie. *Desire and Anxiety: Circulations of Sexuality in Shakespearean Drama*, 71–87. London: Routledge, 1992.

Traub's study investigates the relation between erotic desire and anxiety and how these affect the construction of male and female subjects in Shakespeare's plays. Her monograph is divided into two parts; in the first, Traub examines threats that the female body poses to the male subject. Traub's consideration of *Troilus*, which forms the last chapter of Section One, focuses on the play's conflation of desire and disease, expressed as a military problem in terms of attack and defense. The play's disease, she points out, is syphilis, which the early modern period believed was carried by the itself-unaffected female body and which posed a threat to individual men and ultimately to nations. In *Troilus*, Traub argues, Cressida is the focus of sexual exchange and thus becomes the contaminator. Relating the disease figured as military invasion in *Troilus* to contemporary discourses about AIDS, Traub insists that it is imperative that we find new metaphors for disease that will be free of moral weight.

106. Yoder, R. A. "Sons and Daughters of the Game: An Essay on Shakespeare's 'Troilus and Cressida'." *Shakespeare Survey* 25 (1972): 11–25.

Speaking from the subject position of a post-Vietnam-War American, Yoder calls *Troilus* "our play" (11) and offers a reading which poses large ambitions and rhetoric against disappointing performance and tarnished codes of honor. For Yoder, the public world of honor and "the general state of Troy" (4.2.68) overcome Troilus's allegiance to his private world of love and Cressida. Yoder's Cressida, a child of war, holds fewer illusions than Troilus and is both victim and survivor. When Troilus realizes that he is betrayed, Yoder argues, he sublimates his erotic energy into duty and rages into battle, not recognizing that he, like warriors on both sides, is part of the state at war, "a mechanism that must finally devour itself" (25).

See also no. 165.

F. Stage History; Productions; Performance Criticism; Film and Television Versions.

107. Beale, Simon Russell. "Thersites in *Troilus and Cressida*." In *Players of Shakespeare 3: Further Essays in Shakespearian Performance by Players with the Royal Shakespeare Company*, edited by Russell Jackson and Robert Smallwood, 160-73. Cambridge: Cambridge Univ. Press, 1993.

Beale, who played Thersites in Sam Mendes' 1990 production of *Troilus* in the Royal Shakespeare Company's theaters in Stratford and London, writes of his understanding of the role and strategies he employed to realize that understanding before an audience. Among his many observations on the character, Beale remarks that he is choric, responsible in part for preventing the audience from making easy judgments. On the other hand, he must be untrustworthy in order that his voice not emerge as conveying the "meaning" of the play. Beale played Thersites as a class equal of the Greek warriors, unable to fight because of physical disabilities, and embittered at being side-lined. He admired Achilles, according to Beale, and thus felt anger toward Patroclus. At the play's conclusion, when Thersites's "wars and lechery" vision seems vindicated, Beale believes he is more despairing than triumphant.

108. Beroud, Elizabeth. "Scrutiny of a Mask: A Detailed Account of Shakespeare's *Troilus and Cressida* as Staged and Performed by the RSC at the Swan Theatre, Stratford-upon-Avon, 23rd April, 1990." *Cahiers Élizabéthains* 39 (1991): 57-70.

This article describes a production directed by Sam Mendes, which established locale, provided thematic support, and contributed to characterization by using several relatively simple set devices, including a huge Greek mask, ladders, and curtains. Beroud describes the costumes (black and dark colors for the Greeks, contrasting white and gray for the Trojans) and the lighting effects that divided the mask, suggesting a symmetry between the two sides. However, she found the symmetry modified by the costuming and the stage blocking, which presented the Trojans as a democratic group while suggesting differences in rank among the Greeks. Beroud believes that the credibility the production gave to Pandarus and Thersites as commentators underscored the play's emphasis on disease and corruption, expressed visually in the decaying portion of the mask.

109. Berry, Ralph. *Changing Styles in Shakespeare*, 49-65. London: George Allen & Unwin, 1981.

Berry traces changes in theatrical interpretations of *Troilus* in major post-World War II British productions. He identifies a movement away from the Romanticism of the immediate post-war period (for example, Anthony Quayle's 1948 Stratford production) and away from the nostalgic historical analogy expressed in Tyrone Guthrie's controversial, severely-cut 1956 production at the Old Vic. In the 1960s and 70s—the period to which Berry gives most attention—he reports that the play's titular romance was frequently treated as a sub-plot, its importance subsumed by the consequences of communal appetite, which were emphasized in order to stress themes of anti-establishment, anti-war satire. He also finds the productions of this period (Peter Hall's in 1960 at Stratford; John Barton's in 1968 by the RSC and its revival in 1976; Keith Hack's in 1977 for the Oxford University Drama Society) commonly characterized by full-text scripts, a denial of moral authority in the degree speech (1.3), and a corresponding increase in the authority of Thersites as commentator.

110. **Foakes, R. A.** "Stage Images in *Troilus and Cressida.*" In *Shakespeare and the Sense of Performance: Essays in the Tradition of Performance Criticism in Honor of Bernard Beckerman*, edited by Marvin and Ruth Thompson, 150–61. Newark: Univ. of Delaware, 1989.

Arguing against the view that Shakespeare's plays were performed as economically as possible using the minimum of scenery, properties, and actors, Foakes suggests that, as part of the competition with other London theater companies, the King's Men might well have staged as lavish productions as possible. To support his theory, he examines *Troilus*, noting the need for multiple tents, elaborate torch lighting, processions of heroes in armor, and much public posturing. From his observations on the staging needs of *Troilus*, he finds reason to urge re-examination of other play texts for hints about their staging.

111. **Hodgdon, Barbara.** "He Do Cressida in Different Voices." *English Literary Renaissance* 20 (1990): 254–86.

Hodgdon reads two scenes in *Troilus*—the first and the last in which Cressida appears (1.2 and 5.2)—as a means of examining the gendered gaze. In the first scene Cressida looks on the parade of Trojan heroes returning from battle, and in the second she is looked upon and judged by a series of watchers as she negotiates with Diomedes. By examining the staging of these scenes in a series of twentieth-century productions—Iden Payne, 1936 (Shakespeare Memorial Theater); Glen Byam Shaw, 1954 (Shakespeare Memorial Theater); Peter Hall/John Barton, 1960 (RSC); Barton/Barry Kyle, 1976 (RSC); Terry Hands, 1981 (RSC); Howard Davies, 1985 (RSC)—Hodgdon is able to discuss how cultural reproduction rearranges social meaning as theatrical meaning. Only Davies's production, she concludes, breaks the hegemony of the male gaze and accords some power to a woman's look.

112. Newlin, Jeanne T. "The Darkened Stage: J. P. Kemble and *Troilus and Cressida.*" In *The Triple Bond: Plays, Mainly Shakespearean, in Performance*, edited by Joseph G. Price, 190–202. University Park: Pennsylvania State Univ. Press, 1975.

Newlin undertakes a detailed comparison of the editorial suggestions made in Francis Gentleman's 1774 "acting edition" with the actual editorial decisions made by Kemble in a promptbook for a proposed, though never performed, production at the turn of the nineteenth century. Her study substantiates frequently cited references to the play's lack of popularity and its prolonged absence from the stage, from Shakespeare's own time until the early twentieth century. Newlin's examples illustrate how Kemble's changes worked towards meeting the expectations of his audiences by eliminating comedy, reducing and simplifying rhetoric, restoring heroic stature to classical legend, romanticizing the lovers, expurgating bawdy language, and reordering events to emphasize the war plot and subordinate the love story.

112a. Papp, Joseph. "Directing *Troilus and Cressida.*" In *Troilus and Cressida*, edited by Bernard Beckerman and Joseph Papp, 23–72. The Festival Shakespeare. New York: Macmillan, 1967.

Papp writes of his conception of *Troilus* as realized in the production he directed in Central Park's Delacorte Theater in 1965 (see no. 43). His focus is on the love plot, and he confesses at the outset that he sees Troilus as a "cad" and Cressida as "his victim" (24). "Cressida's downfall," he writes, "is given impetus by Troilus's inability to love" (38). Papp retells the play primarily as it involves the lovers, offering his directorial interpretation of each scene and often comparing Troilus and Cressida to Romeo and Juliet. If Papp's Troilus "thrives on frustration," (46) his Cressida begins as "a little girl trying to act a woman of the world" (58) who is turned wiser and more cynical by Troilus's failure to support her. After the final "disillusionment of the lovers" (66) in 5.2, Papp dismisses the play's remaining eight scenes as "an epilogue of dissonance" (67).

112b. Shurgot, Michael. *Stages of Play: Shakespeare's Theatrical Energies in Elizabethan Performance*, 174–98. Newark: Univ. of Delaware Press, 1998.

Shurgot's book considers how Elizabethan spectators would have responded to the "theatrical energies of several Shakespeare plays" (13). He is especially interested in how selected elements of plays would have been staged in The Theater and The Globe, the specific theaters for which they were written. In *Troilus* Shurgot examines audience response to 5.2, the eavesdropping scene where Troilus spies on Cressida, as staged on the thrust stage of The Globe. He comments that speaking eavesdroppers force the audience to "balance their own reactions against internal comments emanating from the staged action" (175). Working from Sprigg's analysis (no. 113) of the blocking of this scene, Shurgot asserts that Sprigg's perspective privileges Thersites' point of view and thus is too narrow. Shurgot reblocks the scene, Cressida and Diomedes downstage, allowing the audience itself to judge Cressida rather than seeing her simply through either Thersites' or Troilus's "incomplete choric comments that do not attempt to probe the causes of Cressida's anguish" (191). He argues that Shakespeare's "fluid stage" allows multiple perspectives and points of view. The chapter includes diagrams (197-98) of the blocking suggested by Sprigg and the revised blocking argued for by Shurgot.

113. Sprigg, Douglas C. "Shakespeare's Visual Stagecraft: The Seduction of Cressida." In *Shakespeare: The Theatrical Dimension*, edited by Philip C. McGuire and David A. Samuelson, 149-63. New York: AMS, 1979.

Avowedly influenced by J. L. Styan's *Shakespeare's Stagecraft* (no. 27), Sprigg develops an interpretation of the seduction of Cressida (5.2) based, primarily, on those visual and aural aspects of performance that can be deduced from text, including gesture, props, appearance, and physical activity. For Sprigg, the dynamics of stage positioning in this scene mirror the dialectic of the play's larger conflict and create multiple perspectives for the audience. With what he sees as its final and most inclusive view from within the system of "observed observers" and its rapid oscillation in point of view, Sprigg argues that the scene allows the audience to experience the characters' uncertainties.

114. Stamm, Rudolph. "The Glass of Pandar's Praise: The Word-Scenery, Mirror Passages, and Reported Scenes in Shakespeare's 'Troilus and Cressida.'" *Essays and Studies* 17 (1964): 55-77.

As an example of his argument that directors of Shakespeare plays must be attuned to the inner stage directions that appear in characters' speech references to place, time, gesture, and stage business, Stamm looks closely at this feature of *Troilus*. He notes a number of allusions in the speeches to place and time (what he calls "word-scenery"). He goes on to consider "mirror passages," where a character speaks about a gesture or a bit of stage business as he does it. Finally, he examines "reported scenes"—such as the one where Pandarus relates Helen's jokes about

Troilus's skimpy beard—which are only talked about and not played out in stage action. Paying careful attention to these internal signals, Stamm believes, will prevent directors from violating the "inner-form" (57) of Shakespeare's plays.

115. Tylee, Claire M. "The Text of Cressida and Every Ticklish Reader: *Troilus and Cressida*, the Greek Camp Scene." *Shakespeare Survey* 41 (1988): 63–76.

Tylee is concerned with Cressida's character as interpreted by directors' and actors' responses to 4.5, Cressida's arrival at the Greek camp. Quoting contradictory opinions of Cressida, Tylee calls attention to male "blood-lust" (66), which she sees as the central image of *Troilus*. To examine the interpretation of this lust, she looks at several productions which stage the scene where the Greeks kiss Cressida beginning with Tyrone Guthrie's Old Vic production in 1956 and ending with Howard Davies's 1985 RSC production. In general, Tylee finds a revision in views of Cressida beginning around 1970, when more sympathy for her begins to regularly appear. Tylee's final point is that producers need to find a way to dramatize the theme that pursuit of fair appearance corrupts reality.

116. Willis, Susan. *The BBC Shakespeare Plays: Making the Televised Canon*, 229–59. Chapel Hill: Univ. of North Carolina Press, 1991.

Willis's book studies the BBC's production of the complete Shakespeare canon for television. Divided into three parts, it offers a general history and overview of the series; an examination of the styles and choices of the major directors; and a set of production diaries of three individual plays, the first of which is *Troilus* (1981), directed by Jonathan Miller. The production was set and costumed in the Renaissance, and Willis discusses Miller's decision to make the Greek camp radically different from Troy, and to differentiate the Greeks from the Trojans. Troilus and Cressida were to be played as young innocents, and the play staged as a tragedy. Among much else, Willis comments on Miller's commitment to ensemble acting, the rehearse-a-scene-and-shoot method of filming, single-camera scenes, problems in production, time pressures on shooting, comic effects in the Greek camp, and problems editing the video.

See also nos. 28, 30, 35, 36, 43a, 43b, 44, 47, 50.

G. Adaptations; Play as Source for and Influence on Later Writers and Works.

117. Dryden, John. *Troilus and Cressida or, Truth Found Too Late.* In Vol. 13 of *The Works of John Dryden*, edited by Maximillian Novak, 217-355. Berkeley: Univ. of California Press, 1984.

Dryden's adaptation of *Troilus*, published in 1679 and labeled "A Tragedy," makes radical changes in plot, characters, and language (see no. 76 for a comparison of the two plays). Hector's challenge to the Greeks is initiated by prompting from his son, Astyanax, and supported by Andromache. Cressida, considerably less sophisticated and sexually knowledgeable than in Shakespeare's play, demands a promise from Troilus "that the holy Priest shall make us one" (3.2.84-85). Hector tries at length to persuade Troilus to give Cressida to the Greeks for the good of Troy, succeeding only after a fierce quarrel. Calchas instructs his daughter to pretend love for Diomedes so that he will help them both return to Troy; reluctantly, Cressida agrees, and it is her dissembling that Troilus overhears. Hector listens to Andromache's pleas not to go to battle until Troilus persuades him to the fight. Cressida, urged by her father, intervenes as Troilus is about to kill Diomedes, swearing her fidelity to Troilus. When Diomedes contradicts her, she stabs herself. Troilus, realizing too late her truthfulness, kills Diomedes in combat and is then killed by Achilles. Ulysses has the play's final speech "Now peacefull order has resum'd the reynes" (5.2.323), and Thersites reappears to speak the Epilogue.

H. Bibliographies.

See nos. 43a, 43b, 44, 53, 90.

IV. ALL'S WELL THAT ENDS WELL

A. Editions.

118. Fraser, Russell, ed. *All's Well that Ends Well*. The New Cambridge Shakespeare. Cambridge: Cambridge Univ. Press, 1985.

In his introduction, Fraser treats briefly the play's date (c. 1605 by his estimate) and its sources, mentioning similarities with the biography of Christine de Pisan as well as discussing Painter's translation, in the thirty-eighth book of his *Palace of Pleasure*, of Boccaccio's tale from the *Decameron*. Fraser then discusses the play itself, which he calls "a great play whose time has come round" (8). A brief stage history, including productions as recent as the 1980s, concludes the introduction. The play text, printed from the Folio, has both textual and critical footnotes. The volume concludes with a "Textual Analysis" (149-52) that discusses the composition of the Folio and the peculiarities of the *All's Well* text, and argues that it is probably based on Shakespeare's autograph manuscript. A brief critical reading list follows.

119. Hunter, G. K., ed. *All's Well that Ends Well*. The Arden Edition. Cambridge, MA: Harvard Univ. Press, 1959.

Noting that the 1623 Folio is the only available copy text, Hunter argues that it was probably printed from foul papers rather than a prompt text. His policy is to emend lightly the carelessly printed Folio text. He suggests the play's date is likely to be 1603-4, based largely on its affinities with *Measure*. In so dating it, Hunter rejects the argument that *All's Well* is the play which Francis Meres referred to in 1598 as *Loves labours wonne*. Hunter believes that Shakespeare's primary source is Painter's *Palace of Pleasure*, chapter thirty-eight [which Hunter prints as an appendix], a translation from Boccaccio's *Decameron*. In his critical introduction, Hunter discusses the play's problems, singling out Bertram, Parolles, and Helena for particular attention. Rejecting its classification as a problem play, however, Hunter prefers to see it in conjunction with the "later comedies" (lv) or romances. He believes *All's Well* is an early attempt at a kind of drama, "a new poetic vision" (lvi), which comes to fruition in the romances. The text has extensive textual and critical footnotes.

120. Snyder, Susan, ed. *All's Well that Ends Well.* The Oxford Shakespeare. Oxford: Clarendon Press, 1993.

The Oxford edition reprints the Folio text and assumes that at some point the foul papers on which that is based had undergone revision. Snyder's approach to *All's Well*, both in her generous textual annotations and in the detailed introduction, is best captured by her assertion that she has "tried to respond to Shakespeare's rich indeterminacy by opening up possibilities rather than closing them down" (69). Awareness of stage history (the introduction is illustrated with photographs of modern productions) marks the introductory material, which deals with source, dating, the characters of Helena and Bertram, genre, the relationship of the play to Shakespeare's sonnets, and the text. In appendices, Snyder reprints Painter's translation of Boccaccio's tale and extracts on marriage from Erasmus's *Colloquies*.

See also nos. 28, 198a.

B. Dating and Textual Studies.

121. Bowers, Fredson. "Foul Papers, Compositor B, and the Speech Prefixes of *All's Well That Ends Well.*" *Studies in Bibliography* 32 (1979): 60-81.

Persuaded that *All's Well* was printed in the Folio from Shakespeare's foul papers, Bowers examines the varying speech prefixes—especially for the Countess, Lafew, Bertram, and the French Lords—for which the play is notorious. He rejects the possibility that the text has been interfered with by an intermediary, and places the responsibility for the many variations primarily on the author. Using an extended example from the Folio text of *Julius Caesar*, Bowers argues that Compositor B was unlikely to go against copy except for mechanical reasons such as abbreviation. Investigating places where the previous stage direction might have influenced the following speech prefixes, the places where familiarity might lead a compositor to continue a particular form of speech prefix and, alternatively, places where a break either in authorial composition or in typesetting might have caused the author or compositor to break the continuity of the prefixes, Bowers concludes "the compositors were completely conservative in the treatment of names and titles ... and ... copy was followed in these respects with fidelity" (79). He believes the variations to be Shakespeare's own.

122. Bowers, Fredson. "Shakespeare at Work: The Foul Papers of *All's Well That Ends Well.*" *English Renaissance Studies Presented to Dame Helen*

Gardner, edited by John Carey, 56-73. Oxford: Oxford Univ. Press, 1980.

Building from his own conclusions that the variations in *All's Well*'s speech prefixes were Shakespeare's (no. 121), Bowers goes on to use those variations to suggest places where Shakespeare revised his text and to discuss Shakespeare's method of working on a text. Bowers examines altered prefixes in 1.3 and 2.3, concluding that authorial revision is responsible in 1.3 but that interruption in writing is the more likely explanation in 2.3. He also examines three instances of consecutive speeches by the same character, instances of stage directions which call for entrances that actually occur later in the scene, the two versions of the heroine's name—Helena and Helen—and the problem of the two French Lords, whose prefixes Bowers believes get switched (Shakespeare's error he argues) for a time in 4.3. Bowers explains the switch in terms of an interruption in writing by Shakespeare, whose mistake was corrected by Compositor B at his first opportunity after recognizing the error.

123. Cloud, Random. " 'The very names of the Persons': Editing and the Invention of Dramatick Character." In *Staging the Renaissance: Reinterpretations of Elizabethan and Jacobean Drama,* edited by David Scott Kastan and Peter Stallybrass, 88-96. London: Routledge, 1991.

In an essay which argues against editorial regularization of speech prefixes in modern editions of Shakespeare's plays, Cloud (who also publishes under his given name, Randall McLeod) uses the Countess of *All's Well* as his primary example of the losses caused by regularization. Noting that the Folio edition of the play gives this character five different speech tags ("Mother," "Countess," "Old Countess," "Lady," and "Old Lady"), Cloud suggests that the different names may point to stages in the play's composition or to a particular emphasis in a scene. For example, only when Helena is present is this character tagged as "Old," suggesting a youth/age emphasis. Cloud concludes by criticizing editorial *dramatis personae* lists for skewing identities: why is Goneril Lear's daughter rather than Albany's wife?

124. Snyder, Susan. "Naming Names in *All's Well that Ends Well.*" *Shakespeare Quarterly* 43 (1992): 265-79.

Speaking from the position of an editor of *All's Well* (no. 120), Snyder discusses the importance of names, most immediately speech prefixes. Noting that the editorial guidelines for Oxford Shakespeare editors indicate that personal names are preferable to generic ones, Snyder argues for generic names in cases where the names "are casual afterthoughts tacked onto a conception that is essentially generic and functional" (265).

Using personal names for characters who are functionaries in *All's Well*—for example, the French lords, the Clown, and the Countess's steward—reduces the importance of the truly significant names. Snyder discusses Parolles, Bertram and, most important, Helena and Diana as examples of significant names. She associates Helena with Helen of Troy and with the goddesses Venus and Diana, arguing that Helena originally veers between Diana and Venus in imaging herself, but that her ambivalence is resolved when the character Diana appears, representing both Helena's virginal self and unmarried chastity. Snyder speculates that Diana may be about to follow Helena in changing allegiance from Diana to Venus and that the play may offer "a female version of the road to adulthood" (279).

125. **Taylor, Gary.** " 'Praestat difficilior lectio': *All's Well that Ends Well* and *Richard III*." *Renaissance Studies* 2 (1988): 27–46.

Taylor writes as a textual editor to propose emending the editor's dictum expressed in his Latin title—"prefer the more difficult reading"—to "praestat insolitor lecta apta"—"prefer the more unusual apt reading"(41). In arguing his case, he examines several textual cruxes on the first page of the Folio edition of *All's Well*. Because *All's Well* survives only in the Folio edition, he turns to *Richard III* to illustrate how to use his principle when choosing between two variant texts (Q1 and F1).

See also nos. 28, 118, 119, 120, 141, 155, 185.

C. Influences; Sources; Historical and Intellectual Backgrounds; Topicality.

126. **Beauregard, David N.** " 'Inspired Merit': Shakespeare's Theology of Grace in *All's Well that Ends Well*." *Renascence* 51 (1999): 219–39.

Beauregard argues that *All's Well* was written by someone with the "mindset of a Roman Catholic" (235). Focusing on the theology of grace which he finds reflected in the King's miraculous cure due to Helena's "inspired merit" (220) in the first half of the play and in Helena's pilgrimage and prayer in the second half, Beauregard attempts to refute scholars who either deny Shakespeare's interest in theological systems or regard Shakespeare as a conforming member of the Church of England.

127. **Bergeron, David M.** "The Mythical Structure of *All's Well that Ends Well*." *Texas Studies in Literature and Language* 14 (1973): 559–68.

Bergeron suggests that the myth of Mars and Venus lies behind the structure of *All's Well*. As Venus (Helena) triumphs over the reluctant

Mars (Bertram), comedy and regeneration prevail over tragedy and strife. In the course of his discussion, Bergeron explores the relationship of Bertram and Parolles (whom he sees as parodying the military quest) and the Venus/Diana relationship as it was applied to Queen Elizabeth and appeared in other early modern texts and in art. He notes that Helena at first is associated with both goddesses, but eventually the character Diana takes over the association with the goddess Diana, leaving Helena to embody Venus. The underlying myth, he believes, helps readers understand "the contentious nature of Bertram and the generative force of Helena as she heals the King and subdues her Mars" (568).

128. Cole, Howard C. *The "All's Well" Story from Boccaccio to Shakespeare.* Urbana: Univ. of Illinois Press, 1981.

Cole examines treatments of the *All's Well* story, beginning with Boccaccio's *Decameron* and continuing through *Le Chevalereux Comte d'Artois*, Accolti's *Virginia*, and sixteenth-century translations of Boccaccio which reshaped his story (Cole does not translate any of his quotations from Italian and French texts). In his penultimate chapter, Cole discusses topical references—the court, medicine, the military situation in Europe—which may have influenced Shakespeare's play. The final chapter applies this background to a reading of *All's Well*. Cole emphasizes "the story's traditional mischief" and concludes that the play is an ironic reevaluation of a controlling heaven, a kind of religious rationalization, for which he finds precedents in other versions of Boccaccio's story.

129. Cosman, Bard C. "*All's Well that Ends Well*: Shakespeare's Treatment of Anal Fistula." *The Upstart Crow* 19 (1999): 78-95.

Cosman believes that the King's fistula, unlike the thoracic fistula in the Boccaccio source story, is an anal fistula and that its location has implications for staging the play. Cosman first cites the opinions of physicians who have written about the play—which are diverse as to the precise nature and location of the fistula. He then turns to oblique textual references (to ends and buttocks) and scatological imagery as support for his claim. Next, he cites evidence that to Elizabethans fistula commonly meant "fistula in ano," noting that a treatise of that title was written by John Arderne (1307-90), who he says was an ancestor of Shakespeare. He looks at the fistula's placement in the source story and other literary treatments, discusses Charles V's arm fistula, the archetypical non-healing wound of the Fisher king, the chest wounds of Christ figures, and the sick king in alchemy. "By locating the fistula in the anus [Shakespeare] retained both the alchemical aspect of the non-healing wound and the infertility/impotence aspect of a private wound" (90). Cosman assumes that the King's fistula is anal and argues that Scene 2.1 should be staged as "pregnant with low humor, with a smirking Helena and a comically uncomfortable king" (91).

130. Godshalk, W. L. "*All's Well That Ends Well* and the Morality Play." *Shakespeare Quarterly* 25 (1974): 61-70.

Responding to critical arguments that *All's Well* has an underlying morality structure, Godshalk suggests that it may be an anti-Morality in which means are sacrificed to ends, in which Helena, Bertram, and Parolles "are all deceivers" (69). He finds similarities among these three characters, noting particularly what he sees as Helena's moral lapses. "Deceptive means have led to the union of two deceivers" (70). He believes, as well, that the King is morally obtuse. The play, he concludes, is ironic—"a comic Morality Play" (70).

131. Jardine, Lisa. "Cultural Confusion and Shakespeare's Learned Heroines: 'These are old paradoxes.' " *Shakespeare Quarterly* 38 (1987): 1-18.

Jardine's work on humanism and the intellectual history of women has led her to the conclusion that there was considerable ambivalence in the early modern period about "the propriety of imparting humanistic intellectual skills to women" (2). In this article she examines women in two dramatic texts, *All's Well* and *The Merchant of Venice*, whose heroines possess traditional male learning (medical and legal). Jardine finds that Helena's professional knowledge is linked to a sexual "knowing" which threatens to disrupt society. Helena is both the chaste, learned healer and the trickster who ensnares Bertram. According to Jardine, Helena in the second half of the play "atones" (11) for her forwardness in the first half by lapsing into passivity and fulfilling the task set by Bertram. In this reading, Helena reconciles "the opposed figurings of the educated woman as both symbol of civilization and social stability, and 'impudent' " (12).

132. Lewis, Cynthia. " 'Derived Honesty and Achieved Goodness': Doctrines of Grace in *All's Well That Ends Well*." *Renaissance and Reformation* n.s. 4 (1990): 147-69.

Lewis believes that *All's Well* is "a play encompassing a theological tension ... an enigma by design" (167). The theological tension concerns grace: is it given to the elect (Reformation position) or is man able, through works, to partially achieve or deserve grace (Catholic position)? Lewis finds the play embodying both points of view. She also finds Helena, Parolles, and Bertram—all of whom she examines for consistency—characters to whom the audience has ambiguous responses, whose various self-contradictions cause audience sympathies continually to fluctuate. "In essence, *All's Well* insistently winds back upon itself when identifying whether human goodness and grace come from within humanity or from the divine alone" (156).

133. Miola, Robert S. "New Comedy in *All's Well that Ends Well*." *Renaissance Quarterly* 46 (1993): 23-43.

Miola writes about the influence of Roman New Comedy upon *All's Well*, focusing particularly on the *miles gloriosus* figure, which he sees as split into two characters: Parolles as braggart warrior and Bertram as boasting lover. He traces the parallels between their ordeals, exposures, and recognitions. Miola also finds elements of New Comedy in the characters of Helena and Diana and in the motifs of pregnancy and a recovered ring which they introduce.

134. Mukherji, Subha. " 'Lawful Deed': Consummation, Custom, and Law in *All's Well that Ends Well*." *Shakespeare Survey* 49 (1996): 181-200.

Mukherji examines marriage law to determine the significance of Bertram's refusal to bed Helena. Though consent, not consummation, is the signifier of marriage in early modern law, she notes that non-consummation is a chief factor in divorce. Furthermore, consummation was regarded by many—including Bertram?—as a sign of consent, she reports, more personal than participation in an enforced ceremony of marriage. The giving of rings, according to Mukherji, was a material sign of the consent or the consummation which cannot be proved, either theatrically or legally. Helena uses the ambiguities in the law, she argues, to bring about a prudent, pragmatic (if miraculous) conclusion.

135. Powers, Alan W. " 'Meaner Parties': Spousal Conventions and Oral Culture in *Measure for Measure* and *All's Well that Ends Well*." *Upstart Crow* 8 (1988): 28-41.

Powers examines "spousals"—oral private marriage contracts—both in the culture of Elizabethan England and in Shakespeare's plays. He considers a number of examples, including Claudio's "true contract" with Julieta (*Measure*) and Bertram's oaths to Diana Capilet (*All's Well*), which he defines as an invalid spousal. Powers concludes that, though spousals sufficed for marriages in the early comedies, in Shakespeare's later drama oral contracts often represented more formal offstage rites, a change which Powers thinks may mark Shakespeare's own lessening tolerance for folkways.

136. Stensgaard, Richard K. "*All's Well that Ends Well* and the Galenico-Paracelsian Controversy." *Renaissance Quarterly* 25 (1972): 173-88.

Stensgaard argues that Shakespeare's account of Helena's cure of the King relates to contemporary medical debates which had heightened due to the plague of 1603. In his view, the Galenists who had failed to cure the fistula are to be associated with the "establishment" doctors of the Royal College of Physicians and their herbal remedies. Opposed to them were the empirics, unlicensed practitioners, who often espoused the chemical remedies called for by Paracelsus. Classing Helena as an "honest empiric" (190), Stensgaard notes the religious aura associated with her cure, as it was with Paracelsian medicine. Galenists, he argues, were in contrast associated with "the image of the atheistic, pagan physician" (184). Stensgaard suggests that some of Shakespeare's knowledge of and interest in this medical controversy may have derived from John Hall, his future son-in-law, who was himself an unlicensed empiric. Thus, Stensgaard believes that Helena is to be viewed "not from a background of romance storytelling ... but within the aura of moral and social sentiment associated with the [medical] reform movement" (183).

See also nos. 28, 38, 41, 118, 119, 120, 155, 158, 168, 172, 173, 176, 179, 183.

D. Language and Linguistics.

137. Desmet, Christy. "Speaking Sensibly: Feminine Rhetoric in *Measure for Measure* and *All's Well That Ends Well*." *Renaissance Papers* (1986): 43–51.

In the interest of examining the frequent Renaissance personification of rhetoric as a woman, Desmet looks at Shakespeare's two vocal heroines, Helena and Isabella, as examples of the moral ambivalence the period associated with rhetoric itself. From Plato on, Desmet says, certain writers have distrusted rhetoric as deceitful, while others, following Cicero, have seen rhetoric as the proper adornment of an elegant, noble lady. Helena, Desmet argues, wins the King to try her cure more by how she sounds than what she says. He responds to her argument with his senses not his intellect. Similarly, Isabella's verbal appeal to Angelo engages his senses. "In *All's Well* and *Measure*, Shakespeare himself remains uneasy about rhetoric's power to subdue reason and common sense through the ear" (50). Eventually, Desmet concludes, both Helena and Isabella are forced to lie in a good cause, then silenced by male judgments.

138. Hunt, Maurice. "*All's Well that Ends Well* and the Triumph of the Word." *Texas Studies in Literature and Language* 30 (1988): 388–411.

Hunt explores the effect of "the word" in *All's Well* in an attempt to relate speech act theory to Christian doctrine. He highlights the early comments in the play about Bertram's father—a man whose deeds and words supported each other—as an ideal to which other characters should aspire. Hunt discusses Helena's healing language, the King's word which fails to make Bertram love Helena, the riddling words so prominent in *All's Well*, and the "medicinal words" (404) of the Countess's letter and the Rector of St. Jaques's letter to Bertram. At the play's end, Hunt finds a melding of word and deed, last heard in the praise of Bertram's father. "Potentially divine by nature, words in *All's Well* often work propitiously, at key moments through riddles, to fashion a toned-down yet nonetheless authentic happiness for the play's main characters" (390).

See also nos. 144, 146, 160, 161, 166, 168, 172, 183, 189, 198a.

E. Criticism.

139. Adelman, Janet. *Suffocating Mothers: Fantasies of Maternal Origin in Shakespeare's Plays, "Hamlet" to "The Tempest,"* 76–102. New York: Routledge, 1992.

Adelman writes about *All's Well* and *Measure* in a single chapter of her book which examines "masculinity and the maternal body in Shakespeare" (2). In this reading of *All's Well*, Bertram attempts to break away from maternal control by leaving home and then by refusing to consummate his marriage to Helena, the woman supported by and identified with his mother. He expresses desire in another country to another woman only to re-engage with Helena, whom he literally makes a mother. Male power, Adelman argues, is weakened and controlled by female power as Helena controls both the sick King and later Bertram (with the bed-trick). Only by returning to his maternal home and assuming the role of husband, which his mother and surrogate father, the King, have chosen for him, can Bertram acquire full identity as a man. Yet female power is so threatening in the play that Helena is imaged as split: miracle-working virgin and deeply sexual woman. Adelman believes that sex between Bertram and Helena is nearly erased "making her into a dubious virgin mother to protect him from the consequences of her dangerous power" (86). Repr. in no. 279.

140. Asp, Carolyn. "Subjectivity, Desire and Female Friendship in *All's Well*." *Literature and Psychology* 32 (1986): 48–63. Repr. in *Shakespeare's*

Comedies, edited by Gary Waller, 175-92. New York: Longman, 1991.

Using psychoanalytic theory, particularly that of Jacques Lacan, Asp examines Helena, finding her of interest because "she breaks out of both the cultural (historical) and psychic (trans-historical) strictures applied to women in both her time and our own" (177). After surveying the place of women in the Renaissance and in Freudian theory, she turns to Helena as an example of a "new portrait of the female" (180) beginning to emerge at the turn of the seventeenth century: a woman who makes her own decisions. Helena's desire for Bertram motivates her cure of the King, whose patriarchal gift awards her Bertram as legal husband. But to fulfill her sexual desire she must depend on her own cunning and the help of other women. Asp sees Helena as publicly humiliating Bertram in the final act in "anger or rage at having been denied subjectivity by him" (187). By the play's end, Asp argues, Helena's desire has broadened from the strictly erotic to "the larger sphere of female affectivity" (188) and maternal affection.

141. Bennett, Josephine Waters. "New Techniques of Comedy in *All's Well That Ends Well.*" *Shakespeare Quarterly* 18 (1967): 337-62.

Arguing that *All's Well* is closely related to *Measure* and thus written around the same time, Bennett reverses the usual chronology and maintains that *All's Well* was the later play. Comparing the two plays on a number of points—characters, endings, bed-tricks—Bennett suggests that audiences dislike *All's Well* because they see it as a flawed romantic comedy, but that it uses new techniques to deliberately distance the audience from emotional involvement. The play has "no single, unified point of view" (345); it changes scene abruptly and unexpectedly; it delays and then radically shortens the reconciliation scene. Bennett concludes that "*All's Well* marks an advance beyond *Measure* and toward the intricacies" (362) of the romances.

142. Bergeron, David M. "The Structure of Healing in 'All's Well That Ends Well.'" *South Atlantic Bulletin* 37 (1972): 25-34.

Bergeron is interested in how the structure and theme of *All's Well* are united around the idea of healing. He believes the play has a two-part structure: the physical healing of the King (Act 1-Act 2.3) and the metaphorical healing of Bertram and his parodic double, Parolles (Act 2.3-Act 5). Bergeron sees signs of Bertram's cure in his response to his mother's letter, in his understanding of Parolles's bad behavior, and in his apparently sorrowful response to news of Helena's death. He admits that Bertram has a slight relapse as he tries to lie his way out of Diana's accusations, but Bergeron believes that the cure is nearly complete as Bertram vows to love Helena "ever, ever dearly" (5.3.313). The article traces the parallelism of the trick played on Parolles and the bed-trick played on Bertram. Parolles's apparent reform assures the audience of Bertram's reform, Bergeron believes. "To be healed is to have another chance, and this comedy provides that opportunity" (33).

143. **Berthoff, Warner.** " 'Our means will make us means': Character as Virtue in *Hamlet* and *All's Well*." *New Literary History* 5 (1974): 319–51.

Concerned about what he sees as structuralism's emphasis on systems at the expense of character, Berthoff first discusses the importance of character and of "virtue" in imaginative literature. For exemplary texts, he turns in the second half of his essay to *Hamlet* and *All's Well*, detailing their many similarities. He reads *All's Well* as focused on Helena, and as a play about "virtue in use, ... virtue as both champion and prize in a contest of powers where character is tested for its resistance to corruption" (341).

144. **Bly, Mary.** "Imagining Consummation: Woman's Erotic Language in Comedies of Dekker and Shakespeare." In *Look Who's Laughing: Gender and Comedy*, edited by Gail Finney, 35–52. Langhorne, PA: Gordon and Breach, 1994.

Bly notes that the language of physical desire is rarely used in Renaissance comedy, especially by female heroines, and then examines two exceptions: Helena in *All's Well* and Violetta in Dekker's *Blurt Master Constable*. In tragedy, she points out, women may express physical desire and then be punished, but the usual language of love in comedy is petrarchan. In the two exceptions, Bly finds that petrarchanism is debased by the male lovers, who use it for seduction (Bertram to Diana). The heroines' verbal frankness, as they arrange bed-tricks to gain the consummation they desire, "fall[s] outside convention and [is] thus genuine" (47). Because the bed-trick is so explicit, however, Bly feels the plays fit uneasily into the genre of romantic comedy; too realistic to accept instantaneous petrarchan love, they call into question the concluding "true love" of the tricked husbands.

145. **Briggs, Julia.** "Shakespeare's Bed-Tricks." *Essays in Criticism* 44 (1984): 293–314.

Briggs surveys a number of literary bed-tricks, pointing out that they serve two purposes: to win a reluctant husband or to prevent a husband from committing adultery. Shakespeare borrows from these an interest in exploring desire both within and without marriage, focusing on men (Bertram and Angelo) who are attracted to "unattainable" women. Briggs asserts that desire is more threatening to society in *Measure* than in *All's Well*, so that in *Measure* desire must be legislated into marriage. Though the bed-trick is used by Shakespeare to solve the problem of the males' lack of desire for their appropriate mates, according to Briggs, even as Bertram and Angelo are brought back into the community by their marriages, the possibility exists that they can never "desire" the women whom they once rejected as wives.

146. Calderwood, James L. "Styles of Knowing in *All's Well*." *Modern Language Quarterly* 25 (1964): 272-94.

Calderwood summarizes major strands of previous criticism on *All's Well*, concluding that the play is really a "mingled yarn" (275) combining romantic and realistic perspectives. He reads the play as the learning experience of two young people who, through trial and error, acquire "the experience and moral insight needed for the revitalization of a moribund society" (276). Calderwood compares the relationship between Helena and Bertram to that between Shakespeare's Venus and Adonis, aggressive female love opposed to male disinterest and disdain. He also examines the intellectual and sexual connotations of the word "know," emphasizing the connection between sex and knowledge in the play. Pointing out that sex can either devolve into lust or regenerate and rejuvenate, Calderwood compares the King's healing and the bed-trick. Noting the aging of the older generation, Calderwood concludes that Helena has saved Bertram from dishonor by transforming his lust into procreation.

147. Calderwood, James L. "The Mingled Yarn of *All's Well*." *Journal of English and Germanic Philology* 62 (1963): 61-76.

Reacting against readings which highlight "the idealized fairy-tale qualities of plot" (61), Calderwood sets up a series of oppositions for consideration—passive honor vs. earned honor, passive love vs. aggressive love, lustful sex vs. procreative sex—and discusses how Helena and Bertram negotiate these oppositions, producing the "mingled yarn" of their characters and of the play. He discerns two parallel movements in the play's structure, each ending in "the failure of apparent success" (67). Helena cures the King and weds Bertram; Bertram earns honor in war and escapes Helena. Calderwood explains that Bertram lies in Act 5 because he has given away his honor with his ring to Helena. Only when she "cures" him, by revealing that his lustful act was lawful procreation and that his ring is still in the family, can he regain honor.

148. Cartelli, Thomas. "Shakespeare's 'Rough Magic': Ending as Artifice in *All's Well that Ends Well*." *The Centenniel Review* 27 (1983): 117-34.

Acknowledging the problem of closure in *All's Well*, Cartelli argues that the ending is conspicuous for its speed and abruptness, thus enhancing the theatergoer's awareness of the play as artifice. He interprets the King as a frustrated playwright, trying to make all come out neatly, and Helena as another playwright figure, one who is content with a plain, rather than perfect, ending. Noting the simplicity of Bertram's final speeches juxtaposed against the complexity of his earlier lies, Cartelli concludes that Bertram believes in this ending. The King's epilogue confirms the artifice of closure, he argues, giving the audience the gratification of a fantasy fulfilled (though not necessarily believed).

149. Cohen, Eileen Z. " 'Virtue is Bold': The Bed-Trick and Characterization in *All's Well that Ends Well* and *Measure for Measure*." *Philological Quarterly* 65 (1986): 171–86.

Cohen argues that the bed-tricks in *All's Well* and *Measure* promote love and marriage and cause the audience to see the women who devise them breaking the expected pattern of passive behavior. Treating the bed-trick as a form of disguise, Cohen sees Helena and Isabella as heroines who have moved beyond the cross-dressed heroines of earlier comedy. Helena, she says, "saves Bertram from adultery and gives him love" (177), while Isabella's part in the bed-trick is "compassionate and life-giving" (179). The men who agree to the silent, completely dark sexual encounters stereotype women, Cohen points out, never dreaming that the women could trick them. These two heroines, by their participation in the bed-trick, "shock, disorient and ultimately extend a reality" (185).

150. Donaldson, Ian. "*All's Well That Ends Well*: Shakespeare's Play of Endings." *Essays in Criticism* 27 (1977): 34–55.

Taking up Dr. Johnson's comment (34) that the last scene of *All's Well* is "neglected," Donaldson examines the theme of "ending" in the play. He suggests that "endings are continually feared or wished for or spoken of in *All's Well*" (37), and that this results in a skewing of dramatic form—the comedy opens with formal mourning and talk of death, for example. He argues that endings do not always come when characters expect them, that death or "ending" is in the mind of nearly all central characters, and that the play has circular elements which suggest that the end will never come. He also examines "ends and means," an alternative meaning for "end" which the play employs. He concludes that *All's Well* "speaks constantly of an end which is not finally realized within its dramatic framework" (52) and thus resembles the uncertainty of life itself.

151. Ellis, David. "Finding a Part for Parolles." *Essays in Criticism* 39 (1989): 289–304.

Ellis argues against a prevalent critical view that Parolles is a corrupter of Bertram, pointing out his ineffectiveness in that role as well as in his attempts to be a gentleman and captain. After Parolles's unmasking as a liar and coward (4.3), he accepts his role as knave and fool, according to Ellis, and as domestic fool to Lafew is perhaps more "natural" than the play's acknowledged fool, Lavatch.

152. Findlay, Alison. *A Feminist Perspective on Renaissance Drama*, 87–100. Oxford: Blackwell's, 1999.

In a chapter entitled "'I please my self': Female Self-Fashioning," Findlay considers plays "where women's experiences of self-fashioning are central" (88). Among such plays which center on romantic love she includes *All's Well*, noting that Helena both overturns and appropriates petrarchan conventions. She succeeds in her aggressive quest for Bertram, Findlay argues, by enlisting a community of sympathetic females and by fashioning her love from a mixture of maternal and erotic elements. Findlay believes that the play would be especially attractive to female members of the audience as it shows "female conspiracy" which succeeds in breaking up the "all-male camaraderie" (96) of the court world. Noting Bertram's humiliation at being treated as a commodity, the usual female position, Findlay finds the final scene dominated by women characters who know more than the men. "In the re-birth of Helen as the knowing, controlling mother-to-be, female spectators see an affirmation of their own desires for self-expression, agency, and equality in difference" (100).

153. Friedman, Michael D. "'Service is no heritage': Bertram and the Ideology of Procreation." *Studies in Philology* 92 (1995): 80–101.

Using Shakespeare's Sonnet 9 as his starting point, Friedman discusses the conflict between the ideologies of male sexuality in the civilian (marry and procreate) and military (conquer the virgin) spheres. In *All's Well*, the King urges Bertram in both directions, to follow his father as both soldier and family man, yet restrains him from the wars. Parolles, on the other hand, argues that the value of these approaches can be reversed (marriage saps the virility while military "service" can be procreative), but his view is discredited in 4.3. Helena in Act 5, according to Friedman, is simultaneously the deflowered virgin and the spouse who provides the heir, while Bertram is allowed illicit pleasure which turns out to have served his lineal duty to produce a legitimate heir. Looking at performance texts, however, Friedman finds that productions of 5.3 emphasize either Bertram's newly awakened passion for Helena or his attachment to the child she carries, but never both. He believes that, while the conflicting sexual ideologies are often smoothed over in production, the sexual ethics of the father and the soldier are contradictory and remain unresolved in the play's written text.

154. Gross, Gerald J. "The Conclusion of *All's Well that Ends Well.*" *Studies in English Literature 1500-1900* 23 (1983): 257-76.

Examining the scenes leading up to the conclusion, Gross remarks that Helena's romantic vision of Bertram is modified by the play's end, as is her own position as "ideal" romantic heroine by the persistence of her pursuit. Nevertheless, by analogy with the sub-plot—Parolles's acceptance into the court world as Lafew's fool—Gross argues that Helena and Bertram's marriage is foreshadowed as "happy," though in limited terms. Marriage to Bertram is not the ideal envisioned by Helena at the play's beginning or by romantic convention.

155. Haley, David. *Shakespeare's Courtly Mirror: Reflexivity and Prudence in "All's Well that Ends Well."* Newark: Univ. of Delaware Press, 1993.

Haley is interested in reflexivity in *All's Well*—not the individualistic fashioning of self discussed by new historicists, but rather the fashioning of the courtier and his honor. Haley argues that courtiers saw themselves in the larger mirror of the whole court. His primary focus is on Bertram who, he believes, arrives at a court whose sick king is no longer a worthy mirror of honor. When Bertram defies the King's intention (that he stay at home with Helena) and goes instead to war, Haley argues that he demonstrates exemplary "self-transcendence" (44) and heroism. In this reading, Haley finds detailed analogies to *Henry V*, to the biblical story of Ahab (Book of Kings), and to alchemical operations (several alchemical illustrations are included). *All's Well* "is a prudent play that makes a real virtue of preserving one's good name ... [and] dramatizes the court's discovery of wisdom" (238). Haley sees the play as a mirror which defines courtly honor through the good and bad choices made by Helena and Bertram. He also considers at length the roles of Parolles and Lavatch. Haley's appendix proposes an earlier date (soon after 1599) than most other critics, based chiefly on his belief in the play's affinity with *Henry V* and on the likelihood of Lavatch being written for Robert Armin, who probably joined the company in 1599.

156. Halio, Jay L. "All's Well That Ends Well." *Shakespeare Quarterly* 25 (1964): 33-43.

Halio notes the prominence of death and disease in *All's Well*, especially in the opening scenes, and declares Helena "the only healthy thing" (34) in scene one. He sees Bertram as the play's central character, the link between the aged characters in France and the aspiring younger generation whose focus is Florence and the war. Bertram becomes central after his marriage and flight to Florence, Halio argues, when Helena and Parolles struggle for his favor. Halio sees in Bertram's refusal of Helena a parallel to the King's initial refusal of her cure, just as Parolles's self-betrayal is paralleled by Bertram's in Act 5. In the end, he concludes "we ... must accept Bertram" (42).

157. Hall, Jonathan. *Anxious Pleasures: Shakespearean Comedy and the Nation State*, 127–48. Madison, NJ: Fairleigh Dickinson Univ. Press, 1995.

Drawing on Bakhtin, Lacan, Deleuze, and freudian and marxist theorists, Hall reads Shakespearean comedy as representing and implicated in the "schizophrenic" (36) anxieties attendant on the formation of the modern nation state during the sixteenth century. He sees in *All's Well* a struggle between two versions of patriarchy: the feudal notion that honor comes through inherited blood in patrilineal descent, and the centralizing interpretation that the monarch can confer honor and nobility as a reward for "natural virtue." Bertram's disdain for Helena's low birth is pitted, in Hall's reading, against the King's assurance that he can "create" honor and wealth. Only Helena, supported by the Countess, can convert Bertram's resistance into acceptance of the new "natural" order, his lust into honorable procreation. But, Hall acknowledges, audience anxiety is not fully allayed by Helena's restoration of patriarchal order for, thanks to the contrivance this restoration requires, it is no longer possible to believe "that patriarchy is truly produced out of 'nature'" (148).

158. Hodgdon, Barbara. "The Making of Virgins and Mothers: Sexual Signs, Substitute Scenes and Doubled Presences in *All's Well That Ends Well*." *Philological Quarterly* 66 (1987): 47–71.

Hodgdon's analysis deals with three significant threads: Shakespeare's changes to Boccaccio's source tale; "how sexual signs are articulated in characters and events" (48); and the role of "substitute scenes and doubled presences" (48) in the play's narrative. She suggests that some of Shakespeare's changes from the source transform original narrative detail into other forms (Giletta's twin sons transformed "into a series of resonant doublings" [64]). Hodgdon finds Helena's sexual knowledge consistently hidden by riddles or surfaced by Lavatch, whom Hodgdon sees as Helena's double. Similarly, certain important moments which are not staged—the cure of the King, the marriage, the bed-trick—are substituted for by scenes whose language, full of double entendres, refers to those off-stage activities. She concludes that "the play positions women either as virgins ready for marriage or as mothers" (65) and that it ends in compromise, a realistic awareness of the difficulties inherent in human sexual relationships.

159. Huston, J. Dennis. "'Some Stain of Soldier': The Functions of Parolles in *All's Well That Ends Well.*" *Shakespeare Quarterly* 21 (1970): 431-38.

Huston finds Parolles' most notable characteristic to be immense energy. Parolles transforms the mourning palace of Roussillon by his arrival, Huston suggests, and infuses the at-first-passive Helena with the energy which fuels her quest for Bertram. Huston reads Helena and Parolles as struggling for control of Bertram. Helena uses her energy productively, he argues, while Parolles dissipates his destructively; Parolles is "the dramatic actualization of all the King's fears about the characteristics of the younger generation" (437).

160. Kastan, David Scott. "*All's Well that Ends Well* and the Limits of Comedy." *ELH* 52 (1985): 575-89.

After exploring Renaissance definitions of comedy as representations which both reform and refresh, Kastan discusses the formal comic characteristic—the happy ending. The problem comedies, most notably *All's Well*, fulfill the formal requirement of the happy ending, but the audience cannot endorse the ending's contrivance. Kastan examines the play's final scene, where the conditional verbs, Helena's conviction that she has "won" Bertram, and Bertram's overt lies all deeply unsettle the closure. The play's "imperfect" ending, he argues, explores and extends the limits of comedy.

161. Laroque, François. "Words and Things in *All's Well That Ends Well.*" In *French Essays on Shakespeare and his Contemporaries: "What would France with us?"* edited by Jean-Marie Maquin and Michele Williams, 213-32. Newark: Univ. of Delaware Press, 1995.

Laroque argues that *All's Well* dramatizes the distortion of the links between words and the objects they claim to stand for. In a play about sickness, he sees language as sick, "the channels of communication ... dangerously perverted" (214). He finds Parolles most symptomatic of language's perversion; his words are empty with no connection to reality until he is exposed in the drum scene (4.3). Bertram's empty words of rejection to Helena are converted by her into reality: the ring and the heir she carries. Laroque claims that women in the play link words and objects, making words the signatures of things. The play's first half "showed us a world suffering from an inflation of words" (226), Laroque asserts, and the second half searches for a remedy, stressing the importance of things seen—the ring and the revived Helena. Citing Foucault in his conclusion, Laroque claims that the play does not fully paper over the gap between words and things in the early modern period.

162. Leggatt, Alexander. "*All's Well that Ends Well*: The Testing of Romance." *Modern Language Quarterly* 32 (1971): 21–41.

Leggatt argues that the tensions of *All's Well* arise from its form, the deliberate combination of realism and romance. Into a world of decay, he suggests, Shakespeare thrusts Helena, a heroine from romance. "Just as realism, in this play, is pushed to one extreme and becomes sordid, so romance is pushed to the other, and becomes spiritual" (26). Because Bertram is a realistic character, "a shallow, immature young man" (28), Helena must grapple with realistic problems until the final scene, which again calls upon the conventions of romance. "The ending is an honest reflection of the tensions created by the play as a whole" (40). For Leggatt, the play is the work of a courageous playwright who deliberately tests the assumptions of romance.

163. Levin, Richard A. "*All's Well that Ends Well* and 'All Seems Well.'" *Shakespeare Studies* 13 (1980): 131-44.

Acknowledging that critics have split over Helena, interpreting her either as a romantic heroine or as a devious schemer, Levin argues that she is a clever, guileful aggressor. He believes that she carefully lines up a host of supporters, including the Countess, the King, Lafew, and Lord E, to help her accomplish her purpose. Assuming a certain amount of offstage plotting, Levin believes Helena is informed of Bertram's every move and always prepared with a counteroffensive. He hints that her cure of the King is sexual, and that she may not actually be pregnant. In conclusion, Levin suggests that Helena and Parolles are two of a kind, but that Parolles is made a scapegoat—thanks to Helena—while her deceptions remain undetected.

164. Levin, Richard A. "The Opening of *All's Well that Ends Well*." *Connotations* 7 (1997): 18-32.

Levin focuses on the first eighty lines of *All's Well* as they are printed in the First Folio. He is interested in the conversation of the Countess and Lafew, representatives of an elderly upper class "gerontocracy" (18) in *All's Well*. He first reads their lines as showing fortitude, moderation, and solicitude for the younger generation; then he deconstructs those same lines to reveal such qualities as detachment, suspicion, obstructionism, an undue focus on Helena, and neglect of Bertram. Levin discusses the terms of wardship, the nature and location of the King's fistula, and the relationship of a diseased king to an impaired state in early modern England.

165. McCandless, David. "'That Your Dian/ Was Both Herself and Love': Helena's Redemptive Chastity." *Essays in Literature* 17 (1990): 160–78.

As his title suggests, McCandless views Helena as a redemptive figure of "sexually charged chastity" (161). Arguing that *All's Well* is more an early romance than a "defective festive comedy" (161), McCandless develops various similarities between this play and both *Pericles* and *The Winter's Tale*, especially similarities between Helena and both Marina and Perdita, and points to various contrasts between this play and both *Troilus* and *Measure*, especially contrasts between Helena and both Cressida and Isabella. For this critic, Helena combines the romance heroine and the "real" woman in a play he terms "a provocatively open-ended romance" (175). Even the bed-trick, he writes, is not degrading but rather "a mutually gratifying foretaste of conjugal love" (172). Bertram's lack of verbal enthusiasm in the final scene, McCandless explains, is an effective contrast to his earlier effusive lies, perhaps allowing the stage performance "to enhance the credibility of Bertram's repentance" (175).

166. Nevo, Ruth. "Motive and Meaning in *All's Well that Ends Well*." In *"Fanned and Winnowed Opinions": Shakespearean Essays presented to Harold Jenkins*, edited by John W. Mahon and Thomas A. Pendleton, 26–51. London: Methuen, 1987.

In Nevo's reading of *All's Well*, the concerns of the older, parental generation mesh with those of the young. The language vacillates between images of desire and of decrepitude. Helena seeks a (forbidden) father in her love, as Bertram fears a (forbidden) mother. Only when this generational conflict is solved for each, Nevo argues, can Bertram find in the woman he seduced the woman he fled. In its concern with family relationships, Nevo believes, *All's Well* anticipates the concerns of the late romances.

167. Parker, R. B. "War and Sex in 'All's Well That Ends Well.'" *Shakespeare Survey* 37 (1984): 99–113.

Parker begins with Knights's observation (in *The Sovereign Flower*, 1958) of a conflict in *All's Well* between masculine honor (success in war) and feminine honor (chastity). Parker believes that the two views of honor reach an accommodation by the play's end with neither being the ideal it originally seemed. The glories of military service, Parker notes, are qualified by Parolles's shaming and by Bertram's assault on Diana's virginity. Helena's original idealization of Bertram is changed by the scheming and impersonal sexuality necessary to win him. Parker believes Helena is less interested in Bertram by the play's concluding scenes. He discusses the love/war dichotomy in terms of Mars and Venus, particularly as they appear in Veronese's well-known painting. Parker concludes by describing *All's Well*'s "rueful mixture of war and sex, an accommodation of the irascible and the concupiscible ... that remains unsettlingly partial" (113).

168. Price, John Edward. "Anti-moralistic Moralism in *All's Well That Ends Well*." *Shakespeare Studies* 12 (1979): 95–111.

Price argues that Shakespeare portrays the independence of Helena and Bertram as they free themselves from the influence of their elders, unlike the platitudinous action in Painter's version of Boccaccio's tale. Asserting the play's two-part structure, Price finds the opening scenes dominated by moralistic older characters who have Bertram and Helena firmly in check. But as the energy of their language suggests, he writes, both young people move from submission to command. Helena dominates both the Countess and the King through tactful manipulation, but Bertram dominates both the King and Helena by simple denial. In the play's second half, according to Price, Helena emerges as the ultimate victor as she, with her wit, energy, and rhetorical skills, subdues Bertram.

169. Richard, Jeremy. "'The Thing I am': Parolles, the Comic Villain, and Tragic Consciousness." *Shakespeare Studies* 18 (1986): 145–59.

Richard outlines a Shakespearean progression from "comedies of plot," in which characters stay the same and the world relents, to "tragedies of character," in which characters are dynamic in the face of an unrelenting world (145). Within this scheme, the problem plays serve as a transition. Richard focuses on the metamorphosis of the villain, most specifically of Parolles, who discovers that the world resists his efforts to thrive. Associated with empty words, Parolles is unmasked in the drum scene (4.1), and Richard argues that he shows "tragic acceptance" by becoming a humble clown, who speaks the truth but whose words carry no weight. "Aware of the gap between intention and response, [Parolles] prepares us for those tragic personalities who are unable to bridge the chasm between will and conscience" (158).

170. Shapiro, Michael. "'The Web of our Life': Human Frailty and Mutual Redemption in *All's Well that Ends Well*." *Journal of English and Germanic Philology* 71 (1972): 514–26.

Shapiro writes of *All's Well* as a transitional play which presents in embryonic form ideas later to be developed in the romances: children as agents of redemption and an emphasis on "suffering, penance, and contrition" (526). He reads the play as the parallel development of two young people, each needing to achieve something: Helena cures the King; Bertram wins glory in war. In a world dominated by the elderly, Helena and Bertram both make mistakes. Shapiro reads the final scene (5.3) as partially redemptive. He believes that Helena enters defeated, "the shadow of a wife," and that Bertram's spontaneous outburst, "Both, both. O pardon!", reveals his acceptance of her as his wife, turning "a sordid deception into ratification of their marriage bond" (522). Shapiro admits that the serious moral questions raised in the play are perhaps dissolved too easily by the conventions of love comedy.

171. Silverman, J. M. "Two Types of Comedy in *All's Well That Ends Well.*" *Shakespeare Quarterly* 24 (1973): 25–34.

Silverman argues that *All's Well* is a bifurcated play made up of two "irreconcilable dramatic modes" (25). He describes the two modes as naive, miraculous comedy and "one more devious and filled with intrigue" (25). After Helena wins only the external form of marriage with her miraculous cure of the King, Silverman suggests, she turns to new strategies in the second half of the play which are much less full of wonder. The co-existence of the two modes, Silverman argues, forces the reader to re-examine the play's design.

172. Simonds, Peggy Muñoz. "Sacred and Sexual Motifs in *All's Well That Ends Well.*" *Renaissance Quarterly* 42 (1989): 33–59.

Simonds argues that *All's Well* deals simultaneously with both sexual and spiritual matters, a feature especially apparent in its language. Because discussing religion openly on stage was forbidden, she sees the spiritual content of the play as subversive additions which the Renaissance audience would have expected and enjoyed but which darken the play for modern audiences. To support her argument for the period's joining of the sexual and spiritual, Simonds discusses an epithalamion by Catullus, a colloquy by Erasmus, the marriage liturgy established in 1559, the scriptural bedtrick played on Judah by Tamar (Genesis 38), and an Anglican sermon.

173. Smallwood, R. L. "The Design of 'All's Well That Ends Well.'" *Shakespeare Survey* 25 (1972): 45–61.

Smallwood analyzes the major changes Shakespeare made in his source, a tale from Boccaccio's *Decameron*. Shakespeare added new characters: the older generation—who Smallwood finds add an air of "autumnal calm"

(46) and provide sympathy and approval for Helena's quest—and the comics Parolles and Lavatch—who act as foils for the main characters and provide humor. Shakespeare modified the plot; deepened and altered the main characters, Bertram and Helena; and expanded and re-oriented the final scene to emphasize Bertram's self-exposure and the mercy extended to him. Smallwood concludes that the play ends "not in fully achieved happiness, but in hope" (61).

174. Snyder, Susan. "*All's Well that Ends Well* and Shakespeare's Helens: Text and Subtext, Subject and Object." *English Literary Renaissance* 18 (1988): 66–77.

Pointing out gaps in the explanations the dramatic text offers for Helena's actions (after announcing a pilgrimage to Spain, Helena appears in Florence), Snyder looks at the other aggressive female suitor in Shakespeare's drama, Helena of *A Midsummer Night's Dream*. Both Helenas feel shame and unease with their role as wooers, she points out, but in *Midsummer* Oberon takes control of Helena's love affair in proper patriarchal fashion. For Helena's more ambiguous situation in *All's Well*, Snyder offers two contrasting explanations: God (like Oberon) directs Helena's actions, which therefore need no explanation, or the mutual support of a group of women (which Helena lacks in *Midsummer*) strengthens Helena to overcome her shame and pursue her purpose.

175. Snyder, Susan. " 'The King's not here': Displacement and Deferral in *All's Well That Ends Well*." *Shakespeare Quarterly* 43 (1992): 20–32.

Using the brief scene quoted from in her title (5.1)—a mere report to Helena that the King has gone to Roussillon—as an emblem, Snyder examines deferral, displacement, and substitution in the play. The pattern of putting off an expected conclusion exemplified in 5.1 echoes through the play, most notably in 5.3 where, after a series of displacements and deferrals, we are left with Diana's proposed marriage and the relationship between Bertram and Helena strangely uncertain. Snyder traces patterns of displacement downwards (the Clown allowed to speak what the nobler characters cannot say) and displacement upwards (credit for Helena's cure of the King being given to heaven). Snyder also examines "the screen scene" (4.3), which substitutes for the unstaged bed-trick, and notes that Helena's quotation from Bertram's letter in Act 5 differs from the letter as it was read in Act 3. "Veering off, failing to converge and close, is characteristic of *All's Well*" (29), Snyder writes, comparing this quality to a Lacanian description of desire: "at best ... a flawed, imperfect substitute for the image that drives you" (30).

176. **Solomon, Julie Robin.** "Mortality as Matter of Mind: Toward a Politics of Problems in *All's Well That Ends Well*." *English Literary Renaissance* 23 (1993): 134–69.

Solomon suggests that *All's Well* be read in terms both of the transition between Elizabeth's and James's reigns and of the on-going shift in medical epistemology. Making a distinction between Galenic medicine's acknowledgment of the limits of its power (epitomized in the writings of Francis Herring and John Cotta) and the empirics' unlimited hopes for Paracelsian medicine, Solomon argues that the medical debate functions as a metaphor in *All's Well* for the political/cultural struggle between traditional hierarchy and a meritocratic empiricism (articulated, for example, in Bacon's *Advancement of Learning*). Drawing from early modern medical and philosophical texts, Solomon discusses the period's sense of "altered social possibility" (153) and Helena's capacity to pit her knowledge against mortality and thus to alter the boundary of what is possible, both in medicine and in marriage.

177. **Stanton, Kay.** "*All's Well* in Love and War." In *Ideological Approaches to Shakespeare: The Practice of Theory*, edited by Robert P. Merrix and Nicholas Ranson, 155–63. Norwalk: Edwin Mellen Press, 1992.

Stanton associates the love/war connection in this play with words. She argues that the women, led by Helena, defeat the men in all the critical encounters of the play, though Helena must occasionally give the credit for her successes to heaven as a sop to bruised male egos. Helena learns from men throughout the play, finally understanding that she can embody virtue and sexuality simultaneously. The tentativeness of the play's ending (all only *seems* well), Stanton attributes to uncertainty over whether men will accept "rejuvenation of the society through feminine leadership" (163).

178. **Sullivan, Garrett A., Jr.** " 'Be this sweet Helen's knell, and now forget her': Forgetting, Memory, and Identity in *All's Well that Ends Well*." *Shakespeare Quarterly* 50 (1999): 51–69.

Sullivan examines the role of memory and of forgetting in early modern discourse, taking *All's Well* as his chief example. After outlining three models of subjectivity in which memory and forgetting function, he examines *All's Well* and *Romeo and Juliet* in light of his third model, where memory and forgetting intertwine to help constitute sexual desire, which often emerges from "self-forgetting." For Sullivan, to forget oneself is to disengage from the social network, as sometimes happens with drama's desiring subjects. Helena forgets her low station in her desire for

Bertram, forgets her father even as she remembers the medical remedy he has bequeathed her. Her self-forgetting injects desire into the social order. Bertram, in Sullivan's view, is held by the King's memory of his father and by Bertram's own memory of his social position. His self-forgetting occurs when he meets Diana and, in the throes of desire, gives away his memorial ring, symbol of his self-identity. Sullivan reads Bertram not as scheming but inconstant, inhabiting the position of desirous lover only briefly before returning to memory, to his subjection to the King's will and to his marriage. Sullivan finds the play's conclusion problematic because Bertram's love of Helena seems coerced by the King and because the play does not allow us to forget enough to assure us of a happy ending.

179. Traister, Barbara Howard. "'Doctor She': Healing and Sex in *All's Well That Ends Well*." In *A Companion to Shakespeare's Works IV: The Poems, Problem Comedies, Late Plays*, edited by Richard Dutton and Jean E. Howard, 333–46. Oxford: Blackwell Publishing, 2003.

Arguing that *All's Well* combines folkloric plot elements with specific references to contemporary medical practice and politics, Traister focuses on Helen's role as healer, both of the King's fistula and of her own love melancholy or green sickness. Though she allows the King to think of her medical intervention as God's miracle, Traister suggests, Helen is pragmatic in her demand for her fee and in her determination to get Bertram in her bed as a cure for her own malady. Her unqualified success in healing, however, Traister sees as contained and soiled by the salacious comments surrounding her off-stage healing of the fistula and by the worthlessness of Bertram, the marriage partner she has fought to gain. "There is no suggestion that she will ever practice the healing arts again; the troubling female empiric has been erased and replaced by the 'licensed' reproductive wife" (345).

180. Warren, Roger. "Why Does It End Well? Helena, Bertram, and the Sonnets." *Shakespeare Survey* 22 (1969): 79–92.

Warren reads the relationship in *All's Well* between Bertram and Helena as analogous to the relationship between the narrator and his male friend in Shakespeare's sonnets. Warren suggests that Shakespeare may have chosen to dramatize this story because Helena's passion for Bertram allowed him to portray again "the power of love to prevail over all 'alteration' and humiliation" (92). Warren juxtaposes short passages from the Sonnets and *All's Well* to demonstrate their similarities. He admits that the play's ending remains problematic because Helena and Bertram's final scene does not reassure us of their mutual affection, but he believes that Shakespeare "felt that it ended well" (90).

181. **Welsh, Alexander.** "The Loss of Men and Getting of Children: 'All's Well that Ends Well' and 'Measure for Measure.'" *Modern Language Review* 73 (1978): 17–28.

Welsh compares *Measure*, *All's Well*, and Rabelais's *Tiers Livre*, finding in all a reluctance to marry on the part of male characters. He links this reluctance to fear of cuckoldry and of death. In *All's Well*, the focus is on male honor, Welsh suggests, while *Measure* "never effectively separates politics from sexuality" and displays "the problematics of generation not only as they oppress individual choice but as they inform institutions" (22, 23). He sees the underlying problem of generation as unresolved in both plays and views the plays as a transition to the later romances, where the issue of marriage is subordinate to issues of generation, where "daughters are as important as wives" (27). Yet because of the "magic" necessary to achieve the generational reconciliations in the romances, Welsh finds the two problem comedies "more trustworthy" (28) than the romances.

182. **Wheeler, Richard P.** "The King and the Physician's Daughter: *All's Well That Ends Well* and the Late Romances." *Comparative Drama* 8 (1974): 311–27.

Building from the genre criticism of Frye (no. 32) and the psychological criticism of Barber (especially his article in *Shakespeare Survey* 22 [1969]), Wheeler reads *All's Well* as an incomplete step between the festive comedies and the romances. Barber found the biggest change from festive comedy to romance in the relationship between the generations: in *All's Well*, Wheeler notes, the older generation promotes rather than obstructs young love. Wheeler reads the King's relationship to Helena as comparable to the father/daughter relationships of the romances, except that its strong erotic overtones are displaced onto a reluctant Bertram. "Characteristics central to the design of the late romances are present in *All's Well* as intrusions not fully integrated into its comic action" (325). As a result, says Wheeler, the play becomes unsatisfying and even disturbing.

183. **Zitner, Sheldon P.** *All's Well that Ends Well.* Boston: Twayne, 1989.

After the brief recapitulation of stage history and critical history which is standard to the Twayne Critical Introduction format, Zitner examines Shakespeare's alterations to Boccaccio's story, the importance of power and status issues for reading the play, the role of gender and sexuality in making the play "relevant" for modern audiences, and the generational contrasts of the play. Always he emphasizes *All's Well*'s complexity and openness, calling the play "an endlessly tantalizing balance" (150). The final chapter examines the richness of the play's language and structure for theatrical presentation, turning repeatedly for its examples to Moshinsky's BBC production. A brief critical bibliography concludes the volume.

See also nos. 119, 128, 192.

F. Stage History; Productions; Performance Criticism; Film and Television Versions.

184. Bevington, David. "All's Well That Plays Well." In *Subjects on the World's Stage: Essays on British Literature of the Middle Ages and the Renaissance*, edited by David G. Allen and Robert A. White, 162–80. Newark: Univ. of Delaware Press, 1995.

In this informal essay, Bevington reflects on his experience as dramaturg for Nick Rudall's 1989 production of *All's Well* at the Court Theatre in Chicago and the insights which even someone very familiar with the play can have when discussing it with members of a production company. He singles out Act 1.1, emphasizing its many dualities, including Helena's appearance both as quiet mourner and as spirited debater in her encounter with Parolles, a duality Bevington finds central to her character. He examines Act 2.1, noting the centrality of the King, despite his illness, in this all-male scene. Helena's entrance to this court Bevington compares to Joan of Arc's in *1 Henry VI*. In Act 2.3, when Helena chooses from the courtiers, Bevington talks of the blocking. He also discusses the Florence scene (3.7), where Helena and the Widow plan the bed-trick, and concludes with brief mention of the play's final scene (5.3) and its emotional reunion between Helena and her mother-in-law, the Countess.

185. Carson, Neil. "Some Textual Implications of Tyrone Guthrie's 1953 Production of *All's Well That Ends Well*." *Shakespeare Quarterly* 25 (1974): 52–60.

Concerned that many editors dealing with the textual vagaries of the Folio's *All's Well* have never tested their assumptions by seeing a production, Carson uses the promptbook of Guthrie's 1953 Stratford production to look at the staging of certain scenes. Though the Guthrie production made some drastic revisions of the text, Carson believes that the production raised "provocative questions ... about our usual editorial assumptions" (60). His article focuses particularly on stage directions in 2.1 and 4.1, re-assignment of speech headings in 3.5, and the treatment of the French lords sometimes called E and G, whom Guthrie multiplied (on the basis of varied speech headings) to seven or eight.

186. **Dash, Irene G.** *Women's Worlds in Shakespeare's Plays*, 35–63. Newark: Univ. of Delaware Press, 1997.

Studying the promptbooks of past productions of *All's Well*, Dash finds a pattern of cuts, additions, and transpositions which makes the play's strong, confident and aggressive women (particularly Helena and the Countess) seem softer and more traditional. Some of the changes Dash discusses include radical cutting in Helena's conversation with Parolles about virginity; frequent cuts in Helena's soliloquies; an increased emphasis on the Countess's maternal sadness after Bertram's departure for Court; excision of the other courtiers with whom Helena speaks wittily before choosing Bertram; and omission of the pregnancy requirement in Bertram's letter to Helena outlining his conditions. Overall, Dash argues, productions have sought to "mask the nonconformist aspect" (45) of the women's roles in *All's Well*, to make them a more comfortable fit for a patriarchal society.

187. **Friedman, Michael D.** "Male Bonds and Marriage in *All's Well* and *Much Ado*." *Studies in English Literature 1500–1900* 35 (1995): 231–49.

Suggesting that critics should acknowledge the ideological assumptions on which performances are based, Friedman asserts that most performances of *All's Well* and *Much Ado* have been based on the notion of the happy marriage as goal, which often requires non-textual business on stage. For example, stage business often strengthens the claim that Parolles influences Bertram to reject Helena in 2.3 and 2.5, though the text does little to support this reading. Friedman offers an alternative feminist ideology which might produce stagings more attuned to Shakespeare's texts. Noting the pattern of Bertram and Claudio being separated from their male companions before entering into heterosexual relationships, Friedman suggests that these marriages actually forge new bonds with men: "matrimony ... preserves male bonds at the expense of women" (235). In the case of *All's Well*, this pattern means reunion less with Helena than with the King, to whom Bertram addresses most of his closing remarks. By describing productions' staging of Helena's begging a kiss (2.5), Friedman demonstrates his point that an alternate performance text is possible which "foregrounds the significance of male bonding to the institution of marriage in distinct contrast to the modern ideological preference for romantic ties" (244).

188. **Hunter, G. K.** "The BBC *All's Well that Ends Well*." In *Shakespeare on Television: An Anthology of Essays and Reviews*, edited by J. C. Bulman and H. R. Coursen, 185–87. Hanover, NH: Univ. Press of New England, 1988.

In this brief note, Hunter first comments on what he sees as the chief limitation of television production of plays originally written for theater production: loss of the three-dimensionality possible in the theater. He illustrates by looking at the BBC's *Twelfth Night* scene where Malvolio is gulled by Maria's letter. He then turns to examine *All's Well*, which used "mirrors, windows, candlelight, firelight and deep shadow, obliquely angled shots" (186) to emphasize the "composed" quality of the production. He singles out four scenes for comment. In 1.2 the King is discovered sick and in bed, and Hunter sees this staging as a lapse "in a usually cool and contained production" (186). Scenes 4.1 and 4.3 (the ambush and unmasking of Parolles) he compares to the scene with Malvolio, finding them both crowded and hard to follow. He praises the production's last scene, however, noting that Helena's miraculous reappearance is not shown, but that viewers see the "miracle" reflected in the faces of the other characters as they recognize Helena.

189. Hutchings, Geoffrey. "Lavatch in *All's Well that Ends Well.*" In *Players of Shakespeare: Essays in Shakespearean Performance by Twelve Players with the Royal Shakespeare Company*, edited by Philip Brockbank, 77–90. Cambridge: Cambridge Univ. Press, 1985.

Hutchings discusses his role as Lavatch in the RSC's 1981 production of *All's Well* directed by Trevor Nunn. He describes the way the cast attempted to discover the sense of the play's lines and notes that the play's language, though dense and convoluted, has a natural, conversational quality. He describes three types of Shakespearean clown: the simpleton, the servant, and the professional fool. He argues that Lavatch has elements of both the simpleton and the servant, and he stresses the importance of the warm relationship between Lavatch and the Countess. Hutchings sees Lavatch as an unhappy but witty man, torn between good and evil impulses. He explains how he came to play Lavatch as a hunchback and questions whether Lavatch's "love," Isbel, was anything more than a fiction.

190. *John Philip Kemble Promptbooks*, edited by Charles H. Shattuck. Vol. 1. The Folger Facsimiles. Charlottesville: Univ. of Virginia Press, 1974.

A general introduction deals with Kemble as an actor–manager, the first "who systematically published his own acting versions" (xiv), among them twenty-six Shakespeare plays, some plays several times. Shattuck also describes the stage and the "wing-and-flat" system of scene changes (xviii–xxi). Illustrations of famous thespians of the period and of the architectural plans for the Covent Garden Theater are followed by "Professional Annals" of Kemble's career, including two brief attempts to bring *All's Well* to the stage: a single performance on December 12, 1794, with Kemble as Bertram, and two performances in May 1810, with Kemble's brother Charles as Bertram. Shattuck's brief introduction to the facsimile promptbook (the 1811 edition is reproduced) emphasizes changes Kemble made to Shakespeare's text as well as alterations he made to Garrick's version (discussed briefly in no. 192). Most notably, while Kemble continued to omit any unseemly sexual references and reorganize Shakespeare's scenes and verse, he did restore emphasis to Helena and the main plot, reversing Garrick's focus on Parolles and the subplot.

191. McCandless, David. "Helena's Bed-trick: Gender and Performance in *All's Well that Ends Well*." *Shakespeare Quarterly* 45 (1994): 449–68.

McCandless examines how staging the bed-trick might underline the gender instabilities and the erotic subtext which he believes *All's Well* contains. Drawing heavily on psychoanalytic readings, McCandless notes Helena's vacillation between active and passive, "masculine" and "feminine" roles, emphasizing particularly her position as desiring subject and her ability to "perform" femininity. Bertram, he argues, is denied the masculine position and "feminized." McCandless discusses Helena's affinities with the fairy tale heroines of "Cinderella" and "Beauty and the Beast." Staging the bed-trick, he argues, would destabilize the narrative of Bertram's debauchery (4.3) and dramatize female desire. He suggests that Diana might blindfold Bertram—literalizing the darkness and silence restrictions she has imposed and depriving him of the patriarchal privileges of gaze and speech. In such a scene, Helena would become the gazing as well as the desiring subject. McCandless concludes by discussing the uncertain success of the Act 5 reconciliation between Helena and Bertram. "Modern performance could underline Helena's and Bertram's status as subjects-in-progress, active agents inextricably engaged with subjugating myths of gender" (468).

192. Price, Joseph G. *The Unfortunate Comedy: A Study of "All's Well that Ends Well" and its Critics*. Toronto: Univ. of Toronto Press, 1968.

Price's book provides a stage and critical history of *All's Well* to 1964 and concludes with his critical "defense" of the play. In the eighteenth century, the play was presented as a farcical vehicle for Parolles and, in Garrick's adaptation, Helena became a passive, background character. In the few nineteenth-century productions, Price contends, Kemble's adaptations transformed it to a melodrama dominated by a sentimental Helena. The twentieth century sought realism, according to Price, and its productions searched for a unifying conception. Price also examines American and minor productions, concluding that a definitive production had not yet been staged. Criticism of *All's Well* roughly paralleled its stage history, according to Price: emphasis on comedy and farce in the eighteenth century, sentiment and romance in the nineteenth, and psychological realism in the twentieth. Early twentieth-century critics deemed the play a failure, while those writing between 1940 and 1964 were more favorably disposed. Price believes that *All's Well* is successful as a multi-toned, multi-genred drama which is not susceptible to a single, unified critical conception.

193. Richards, Kenneth. "Samuel Phelps's Production of *All's Well That Ends Well*." In *Essays on Nineteenth Century British Theater*, edited by Kenneth Richards and Peter Thomson, 179-95. London: Methuen, 1971.

Noting that Samuel Phelps's 1852 production of *All's Well* has received little critical attention, Richards remarks on the bravery of Phelps's attempt to revive a play with an indelicate plot and spotty stage history. After a brief discussion of Phelps's policies at his Sadler's Wells Theater and a brief stage history of *All's Well* before 1852, Richards discusses Phelps's production which was based on Kemble's 1811 edition (see no. 190). Highly edited and cut to avoid offending, Kemble's text presents a "romantic and sentimental melodrama, with Helena its focus as the pathetic victim of scorned love" (184). The production itself—as suggested by the surviving promptbook—was formal with little stage business. Phelps played Parolles to critical acclaim, but his production remained balanced and, according to Richards, was praised for its ensemble work. Richards speculates that Phelps was attempting—in a period increasingly addicted to submerging text beneath production details—to return to emphasis on the spoken word, to what nineteenth-century criticism terms "elocutionary" (194) production.

194. Rutter, Carol. "Helena's Choosing: Writing the Couplets in a Choreography of Discontinuity (*All's Well that Ends Well* 2.3)." *Essays in Theatre* 9 (1991): 121-39.

Rutter offers a feminist reading of 2.3, focusing on Helena's positioning and actions and asserting that Helena has affinities, not with Shakespeare's other heroines, but with male characters "who know what they want and go about to get it" (122). In the scene, Rutter discusses Helena's delayed entrance, the stage direction which has her enter dancing, and her control of the choosing (in rhymed couplets). She then examines 2.3 in two Royal Shakespeare Company productions: a 1981 production directed by Trevor Nunn and a 1989 production directed by Barry Kyle, with occasional references to the 1980 BBC production. Nunn's Edwardian production gave Helena the opportunity to play her role freely, showing her transformed by her successful cure of the King until refused by the immature Bertram, who was clearly out of step with the rest of the court. In Kyle's production, "set in the nursery of Bertram's memory" (134), Helena does not fare so well, Rutter argues. Her lines are cut; she interacts with only two suitors before Bertram (both are relieved not to be her choice). Bertram's aversion is thus generalized to the whole court and—despite Kyle's addition of women characters to support Helena as she moves from Italy back to Roussillon—Rutter believes a feminist reading is "sabotaged" by Kyle's production choices.

195. Styan, J. L. *All's Well that Ends Well.* Shakespeare in Performance. Manchester: Manchester Univ. Press, 1984.

One in a series which studies individual plays as they have been realized in production, Styan's volume begins with an overview of the play's central issues: its scanty early performance history; its genre; its "sensitive topics" (11) including the bed-trick; the characters of Helena, Bertram, and Parolles; the theme of youth and age. Within each of these discussions Styan illustrates his points by citing individual productions or actors' interpretations of the question being examined. In the second part of his text, Styan writes a scene-by-scene discussion, sometimes even breaking scenes into smaller units for analysis. Within each unit, Styan refers to reviews or production notes to illustrate ways in which particular moments have been played. Included are eight illustrations of productions from the 1950s through the 1980s. This small volume ends with an appendix listing the dates, locations, and directors of eighteen twentieth-century productions, and the principal casts of fifteen of those productions. The volume is indexed, though character names are not included in the index.

196. Styan, J. L. "The Opening of *All's Well That Ends Well*: A Performance Approach." In *Entering the Maze: Shakespeare's Art of Beginning*, edited by Robert F. Willson, Jr., 155–67. New York: Peter Lang, 1995.

Styan is interested in the verbal and visual clues in the opening scene of *All's Well*, which he believes signal the playwright's intention. Among these he remarks on the opening prose (and later a significant shift to poetry); the mournful scene with all characters dressed in black; Helena's initial silence and separation from the other characters; potential tension from Bertram as the attention turns toward Helena and away from him. Styan believes that the play has "two levels" (164), and that it is incumbent upon any production "to incorporate both the realistic/psychological and the romantic/visionary view" (166). He finds this balance apparent in the opening scene.

197. Warren, Roger. "Some Approaches to *All's Well that Ends Well* in Performance." In *Shakespeare, Man of the Theater: Proceedings of the Second Congress of the International Shakespeare Association, 1981*, edited by Kenneth Muir, Jay L. Halio, and D. J. Palmer, 114-20. Newark: Univ. of Delaware Press, 1983.

Warren begins with the premise that one should look at a production for what new understanding it can give about a play. He focuses primarily on Tyrone Guthrie's 1959 production at Stratford and Moshinsky's 1980 BBC production, with brief excursions into Michael Benthall's 1953 Old Vic production (which lightened and simplified the play, revealing "Helena as Cinderella" [115]) and Trevor Nunn's 1981 Stratford production (called "intimate," "tender," and "conversational" [120]). Guthrie's Edwardian production emphasized class, Warren reports, and made the characters as realistic as possible, with Helena's cure of the King staged as a sort of word charm, almost magic. The BBC production, in contrast, stressed the sexual element in Helena's power over the King's illness. Warren praises the final scene of Moshinsky's production, which focused on the characters' reactions to Helena's reappearance, especially that of Bertram "to whom she now appears a deliverer"(119).

198. Willis, Susan. "Making *All's Well That Ends Well*: The Arts of Televised Drama at the BBC." In *Shakespeare and the Arts*, edited by Cecile Williamson Cary and Henry S. Limouze, 155-63. Washington: Univ. Press of America, 1982.

Willis discusses Elijah Moshinsky's 1980 production of *All's Well* for the BBC. Stressing a strong visual sense of the period, he chose sets and costumes adapted from sixteenth- and seventeenth- century art, especially emphasizing chiaroscuro effects. Willis points out that the play's twenty-three scenes were expanded to thirty-two in this production, mostly by breaking up long scenes to give a sense of more time passing. She remarks on the beauty of some of the small, often unnoticed scenes in Moshinsky's production, and details certain changes from the play's text and certain repeated stage motifs (such as a mirror fascination for Parolles and Bertram). She comments on a kiss Bertram gave Helena in Act 5 and on the King's delivery of the play's final couplet. Willis ends by emphasizing "the sense of tradition—in painting, theatre, and film—evident" (162) in the production.

See also nos. 28, 30, 35, 36, 118, 120, 129, 153, 183.

G. Pedagogy.

198a. Huddlestone, Elizabeth, and Sheila Innes, eds. *All's Well That Ends Well*. Cambridge School Shakespeare. Cambridge: Cambridge Univ. Press, 1993.

One of a series of Shakespeare volumes "specially prepared to help all students in schools and colleges" [iv], this edition prints the full text of the New Cambridge Shakespeare *All's Well* (see no. 118). Facing each page of text is a single sentence summary of what happens on the text page, glossary notes, and suggestions for activities to highlight textual details. Many production photographs are included. The final pages of the volume briefly treat topics such as the play's language, social class and gender, Helena's character, and the play's staging. For each of these topics questions and activities are suggested.

H. Bibliographies.

See nos. 118, 183.

V. MEASURE FOR MEASURE

A. Editions.

199. Bawcutt, N. W., ed. *Measure for Measure.* The Oxford Shakespeare. Oxford: Clarendon, 1991.

In his introduction, Bawcutt suggests that the topical allusions in *Measure* are not distinct enough to firmly date its composition, to identify the Duke with King James, or to interpret the play as a vehicle for royal education. Information about Renaissance marriage contracts is contextualized in a discussion of cultural pressures to regulate sexuality. Detailed comparisons are made between *Measure* and its sources. An extensive performance history, from Davenant's adaptation to a post-Cultural Revolution production in China, is supplemented with illustrations. Bawcutt extends the concept of *Measure* as a "problem play" beyond its ethical and moral themes to include the artistic problems which affected Shakespeare's presentation of character and the problem of unresolved questions in the play's open-ended outcomes, most notably in Isabella's failure to respond to the Duke's proposal. The textual introduction discusses competing arguments for foul papers or for promptbook as the scribe's source and identifies places in the text which have suggested revision to some critics. Bawcutt concludes that the source for the folio was foul papers and provides "missing" stage directions. He chooses F1 as copy text, modernizing spelling and adding selected textual notes and scholarly commentary as footnotes. Appendices provide longer textual notes, alterations to lineation, and a musical transcription of "Take, O Take" with notes. The introduction and commentary are indexed. For a description of the series, see no. 12.

200. Eccles, Mark, ed. *Measure for Measure.* A New Variorum Edition of Shakespeare. New York: Modern Language Association, 1980.

Eccles prints the First Folio text accompanied, on each page, by textual notes indicating significant differences in subsequent editions and by commentary, including previous scholarly annotations, designed to explain its language and action. Line numbering corresponds to the Norton facsimile of F1 and to that of the *Oxford Shakespeare Concordances.* Globe edition act-scene-line numbers are also given. A detailed appendix discusses composition, printing and stage histories, sources, analogues, influences, and music. Eccles prints, as likely sources, George Whetstone's *Promos and Cassandra* and his novella in *Heptameron*, as well as a translation of Giraldi's *Hecatomithi*. Brief extracts from influential criticism are listed chronologically within subject categories. The appendix is followed by an extensive bibliography and a detailed index. For a description of the series, see no. 8.

201. Gibbons, Brian, ed. *Measure for Measure.* The New Cambridge Shakespeare. Cambridge: Cambridge Univ. Press, 1991.

In his introduction, Gibbons discusses how the play's edict making fornication a capital offense reflects real proposals of English Puritan extremists. He finds similarities to King James in the characterization of the Duke. In addition to the play's accepted sources by Giraldi and Whetstone, Gibbons discusses James's interest in the ethics of rule and his treatise, *Basilicon Doron*, the disguised ruler in Whetstone's *A Mirrour for Magistrates of Cyties*, Elyot's *Image of Governaunce*, Middleton's *The Phoenix*, and Marston's *The Malcontent*, the pastoral tragi-comedy of the Mariana plot as derived from the *Decameron*, and relationships to Jonson's *Sejanus*. Gibbons argues that the interrelationship of the polarized comic and serious plots provokes audiences to rethink their responses, that the concept of exchange is presented as central to the relationship of love and commerce, and that Shakespeare gave the Duke multiple occasions to feel "what wretches feel, if only briefly" (39). A detailed stage history begins with Davenant's adaptation, which initiated the long-standing tradition of excising the "vulgarities" from *Measure*, and ends with Nicholas Hytner's sordid 1988 production. Performance photos, paintings, and drawings illustrate the introduction. Textual and content notes appear as footnotes. A "Textual Analysis" discusses the original F1 printing and transcription of the play, with attention to the characteristic traits of Ralph Crane, the play's recognized scribe, and to diluted oaths, discrepancies in context and time scheme, and difficulties in distinguishing verse from prose lineation. A short reading list is included. There is no index.

202. Lever, J. W., ed. *Measure for Measure.* The Arden Edition of the Works of William Shakespeare. London: Methuen, 1965.

Lever's comprehensive introduction includes a discussion of the textual history of the play, explaining the process and value of textual study. He views the "widespread anomalies and corruptions" (xiii) which previous editors have found in *Measure* as less pervasive and characteristic than most do. Shakespeare's treatment of time and plot, the presence of redundant, mute and near-mute characters, and textual anomalies of several sorts are analyzed to refute the claim that *Measure* is an often revised and corrupt text. Consistent with his opinion that behind the F1 text is "Shakespeare's own rough draft, in reasonably good condition" (xxxi), Lever dates the composition of the play, largely through reference to topical allusions, between May and August 1604. Lever's discussion of source materials is informed by consideration of three plot components: "the Corrupt Magistrate," "the Disguised Ruler," and "the Substituted Bedmate," each of which is drawn from a "wide alluvial tract of literary and historical influences" (xxxv). For Lever, the Duke's use of quasi-divine power, even to teach virtue, ultimately deprives his subjects of autonomy and himself of full humanity. This editor sees *Measure* as a "flawed masterpiece" when viewed alone, but as something more when it is recognized as a step towards later plays which confront the dilemma of "authority vested in flesh and blood" (xcvii). The modern spelling text is accompanied by extensive textual, glossarial, and critical footnotes. Appendices include a 1547 letter from a Budapest archive outlining events bearing on the plot, extracts from sources by Giraldi and Whetstone, and a musical transcription of "Take, O Take," with a summary of research on the music. A general description of the Arden editions appears in no. 10.

See also nos. 28, 265, 275.

B. Dating and Textual Studies.

See nos. 28, 199, 201, 202, 253.

C. Influences; Sources; Historical and Intellectual Backgrounds; Topicality.

203. Astington, John H. "The Globe, the Court and *Measure for Measure*." *Shakespeare Survey* 52 (1999): 133-42.

This article suggests that *The Fair Maid of Bristow*, a play performed at Hampton Court before the King by the King's Men at Christmas, 1603, influenced Shakespeare as he wrote *Measure*, particularly Act 5. Astington notes that *The Fair Maid* contains, among much else, a character disguised as a friar who suddenly is unhooded to reveal his true identity, a prison scene, and a heroine who—though badly misused by her husband—nevertheless defends him and prays for his pardon. Astington believes that *The Fair Maid*, freshly in Shakespeare's memory from its Court performance, influenced his composition of *Measure*, probably written in 1604 and staged at Court during the Christmas season of that year.

204. Battenhouse, Roy. "*Measure for Measure* and Christian Doctrine of the Atonement." *PMLA* 61 (1946): 1029–59.

Battenhouse's influential article begins with a declaration of method: "discriminating the patterns by which Christian ethics and Christian art declare themselves; and then testing the relevance of such patterns to the actual texture of Shakespeare's drama" (1031). To do this, Battenhouse points out parallels between the Christian Atonement narrative and *Measure*. He then recounts certain theological scenarios—the hook and line with which God fishes for sinners, the ransom which must be paid to redeem those whom the devil has ensnared, and the espousal of Christ to the Church—and concludes that "the whole pattern of [*Measure*] depends ultimately on Christian myth" (1054). Battenhouse points out that the two major changes Shakespeare makes to his primary source, Whetstone's *Promos and Cassandra*, are the Duke's role in disguise and the Mariana episode, both of which draw the play more into alignment with the Atonement doctrine. Battenhouse believes that Shakespeare did not necessarily set out to write an Atonement parable, but that it emerged as he set Whetstone's plot materials within a Christian culture.

205. Bennett, Robert B. *Romance and Reformation: The Erasmian Spirit of Shakespeare's "Measure for Measure."* Newark: Univ. of Delaware Press, 2000.

As its title suggests, Bennett's monograph reads *Measure* through the lens of Erasmian humanism, arguing that drama can serve as a vehicle for social reform. Generally, Bennett follows earlier Christian allegorists such as Knight (no. 244) and Battenhouse (no. 204), but he acknowledges, and to some extent engages, the skeptical, post-modern critiques of the play which dominate the last half of the twentieth century. Bennett believes that *Measure* is a comic romance, a genre which affirms providential nature, provided in the play by the mentoring of the Duke. Isolating fornication and calumny as the social problems addressed by *Measure*, Bennett examines London in 1604 as a factionalized society which threatened humanist theater's curative agenda. In this context, he sees *Measure* as developing a contrast between a humanist Duke and two rigid idealists, Angelo and Isabella, characters whom he associates with the English Puritans. Bennett sees the dialectical, non-coercive nature of the humanist movement exemplified in the Duke's proposal to Isabella. Her choice to wed him or not remains open just as, Bennett argues, the audience's choice of attitude toward the issues the play has raised remains open in true humanist fashion.

206. Bernthal, Craig A. "Staging Justice: James I and the Trial Scenes of *Measure for Measure.*" *Studies in English Literature 1500–1900* 32 (1992): 247–69.

Bernthal discusses the 1603 treason trials of Markham, Grey, Cobham, and Raleigh, emphasizing the deliberate staging of James's dramatic pardon of the first three men as they stood on the scaffold and the delay of Raleigh's death sentence. Bernthal suggests that these events are echoed some six months later in *Measure* when Vincentio stages the pardons of Claudio, Angelo, and Barnardine, noting that, just as the evidence against Raleigh was extremely tenuous, so Angelo had really committed no crime for which he could be hanged. These parallels permit readings, Bernthal asserts, which either are pro-James—the exemplar of justice tempered by mercy—or which, cynically, see the play as an exploration of how power can be staged.

206a. Cox, John D. "The Medieval Background of 'Measure for Measure.'" *Modern Philology* 81 (1983): 1–13.

Arguing that *Measure* has affinities with medieval dramatic traditions, Cox looks specifically at plays dealing with sexual misconduct (most notably in the N-Town cycles of mystery plays). He examines particularly the contrast between "old law" and "new" (2) in plays about Mary and Joseph and the woman taken in adultery, and discusses the theme of sovereignty in plays about Mary Magdalene. Cox finds echoes of similar themes and treatments in *Measure*, but also sees innovation and adaptation in Shakespeare's play. Shakespeare portrays a human Duke rather than a god figure, and creates an opponent, Lucio, who is more than an abstraction and who generates comic sympathy. Cox concludes that *Measure* "owes more dramaturgically to the medieval convergence of the sublime and the humble than it does to heroic Jacobean magnifications of the monarchical image" (13).

207. Cunningham, Karen. "Opening Doubts Upon the Law: *Measure for Measure.*" In *A Companion to Shakespeare's Works IV: The Poems, Problem Comedies, Late Plays*, edited by Richard Dutton and Jean Howard, 316–32. Oxford: Blackwell Publishing, 2003.

Briefly rehearsing the paradoxical critical evaluations of *Measure*, Cunningham asserts that the play is linked to "a seventeenth-century legal ritual: the practice of mooting" (317). As practiced in the Inns of Court, moot cases involved legal problems which were debated by students who were encouraged to imagine all sorts of mind-stretching contingencies and exceptions. Its purpose was "to show how legal principles might work in hypothetical situations" (319). Cunningham shows how the twists and turns of *Measure*, its patterns of change, its refusal of closure, resemble mooting. She reads the Duke not as a semi-divine ruler but as a figure whose control is partial and temporary and whose apparent success is bred of coincidence. *Measure*, she concludes, forges "communal identities, accustoming audience members to ways of thinking about the conjectural, the arbitrary, the improbable" (328).

208. **Goldberg, Jonathan.** *James I and the Politics of Literature: Jonson, Shakespeare, Donne & their Contemporaries*, 230-39. Baltimore: The Johns Hopkins Univ. Press, 1983. Repr. in Wheeler (no. 279).

In this new historicist reading of *Measure*, Goldberg asserts that the essential link between politics and literature in the Jacobean period is representation. In *Measure*, the Duke's powers are those of sovereign and playwright, for he "authors and authorizes" (232) the actions of the play's other characters. Like James, Goldberg says, the Duke rules through a presence-in-absence stance, which allows him alone, as looker-on, divine status. *Measure* makes visible the nature of Vienna's government, he argues, revealing the politicization of the body, the link between private and public.

209. **Greenblatt, Stephen.** *Shakespearean Negotiations: The Circulation of Social Energy in Renaissance England*, 137-42. Berkeley: Univ. of California Press, 1988.

The few pages in which Greenblatt considers *Measure* appear in the midst of a chapter discussing the arousal and manipulation of anxiety by the State and by the theater in early modern England. In the State, "salutary anxiety ... blocks the anger and resentment"(138) against a seemingly unjust rigor and, once allayed, gives way to loyalty and obedience. In the theater, salutary anxiety is meant to give way to pleasure. In *Measure*, Greenblatt argues, this strategy is examined in the disguised Duke's conversations with the pregnant Juliet and with the condemned Claudio in prison. Neither of these conversations in which he declares that Claudio must die produces the theological repentance which Vincentio hopes to spark, but the arousal of anxiety does produce pleasure in the spectators, writes Greenblatt, and "that pleasure is precisely Shakespeare's professional purpose" (142).

210. **Hammond, Paul.** "The Argument of *Measure for Measure*." *English Literary Renaissance* 16 (1986): 496-519.

Hammond's purpose is to look at the "argument" of *Measure* and examine the play's various arguments about justice. He finds the validity of those arguments called into question, and notes the presence of a subversive response to the source material the play adapts. Highlighting relationships between James's own published writings and passages in *Measure*, as well as the political instability of his new court, Hammond concludes that the play is deliberately unstable. He argues that the play calls attention to the limitations of comic form and rational argument to deal with the complexities of human nature.

211. **Hayne, Victoria.** "Performing Social Practice: The Example of *Measure for Measure*." *Shakespeare Quarterly* 44 (1993): 1-29. Repr. in Wheeler (no. 279).

This essay begins with the observation that *Measure* stages certain social practices having to do with betrothal, marriage, and adultery. Hayne examines the rituals of betrothal, the treatment of prenuptial pregnancy, the Puritan interpretation of the laws against fornication, and the theatrical convention of the disguised friar, illuminating the exchanges negotiated between social practice and theatrical representation in this play.

212. **Lupton, Julia Reinhard.** *Afterlives of the Saints: Hagiography, Typology, and Renaissance Literature*, 110-49. Stanford: Stanford Univ. Press, 1996.

Lupton's book examines how motifs and conventions drawn from saints' lives are incorporated in medieval and early modern secular literary works. In her chapter "Saints on Trial," she considers Isabella and Angelo as characters in two overlaid hagiographic scenarios: the martyred virgin persecuted by tyrannical authority and the ascetic hermit tempted by the devil as woman. To the contradictions imposed by these competing hagiographic traditions, she attributes the play's status as a problem play. Lupton relates this double hagiography to the novella tradition and argues that, just as Isabella moves between the positions of martyr and devil, so she moves between advocacy of mercy and of justice. Though the saint confronted by the tyrant eventually dominates the narrative of *Measure*, Lupton suggests that the alternate hagiography of feminine diabolism reemerges in critics' frequent condemnation of Isabella. Lupton considers Isabella's relation to the law in terms of the psychoanalysis of religious typology, concluding that her rejection of Claudio "is not an eccentric, irrational reaction, but the consummation of her identification with the law in its dead and killing letter" (134), a position Isabella revises in Act 5 when she again pleads for mercy. Lupton also considers decapitation—an emblem of hagiography—as it is used literally and metaphorically in *Measure*. Barnardine alone resists the substitutions rampant in the play by not taking the place of another.

213. Marcus, Leah S. *Puzzling Shakespeare: Local Reading and Its Discontents*, 160–202. Berkeley: Univ. of California Press, 1988. Repr. in Wheeler (no. 279).

Marcus discusses the relationship of James I's London to the Vienna of *Measure*, noting similar problems and governmental responses to those problems. If the Vienna of *Measure* is read as London, she argues, then the play displays "a ruler who succeeds in establishing equity and a semblance of social order when his deputy has spectacularly failed" (164), but if Vienna is *not* London, then the play can be read as "a dark fantasy of alien Catholic domination" (164). Among the topics Marcus treats are the relationship between a ruler and his deputies, jurisdictional conflicts over the interpretation of law, attitudes toward fornication, and possible English counterparts of Shakespeare's characters (Angelo's likeness to Chief Justices Popham and Edward Coke; Vincentio's similarity to James I). She suggests that the play stages the City's desire for autonomy against James's desire for imperial control. In Marcus's reading, Isabella may have a symbolic relationship to Elizabeth I or to the City of London itself, reluctantly forced into a marriage with James I.

214. Mullaney, Steven. *The Place of the Stage: License, Play, and Power in Renaissance England*, 88–115. Chicago: Univ. of Chicago Press, 1988.

In a chapter which discusses "exemplary power"—demonstrations intended to showcase power and to persuade the citizenry of their role in its functioning—Mullaney chooses *Measure* as his exemplary theatrical text, placing it in a cultural lineage which began with Machiavelli's *The Prince*. Claiming that power in early modern England was increasingly theatricalized, Mullaney reads Isabella's confession of sexual shame in Act 5 as her submission to the secular patriarchy. Mullaney sees *Measure* as responding to the transition of power from Elizabeth to James by exploring how a more intrusive form of power might operate; even such power, however, had limits (as Barnardine's refusal to submit to the Duke's will suggests). Against Isabella and Angelo, Mullaney finds the Duke's exemplary power effective, as it shatters their sense of self. "The power of the stage was precisely the power of fiction, the power to induce an audience or an Angelo to view themselves as actors in their own lives, as artificial and artfully manipulated constructions . . . whether they were constituted by a playwright or by larger cultural forces of determination" (113).

215. Scott, Margaret. " 'Our City's Institutions': Some Further Reflection on the Marriage Contracts in *Measure for Measure*." *ELH* 49 (1982): 790–804.

Responding to the scrutiny that English law and marriage contracts have received from critics of *Measure*, Scott points out that the play's law is story-book law, kept deliberately vague. If the setting is Catholic Vienna, then the laws governing marriage are those passed in 1563 by the Council of Trent, which declared handfast or clandestine marriages invalid. An English audience, she argues, while perhaps aware of this Catholic interpretation of marriage, would also have been aware that in England such pre-contracts were valid, though blameworthy. Scott believes that this double view of the relationships between Claudio and Julietta and Mariana and Angelo would have added to the multiple ambiguities of the play. She argues that the Duke and Isabella alter their attitude toward such relationships: first condemning Claudio and Julietta but later approving of Mariana's night with Angelo as "no sin," and that their very inconsistency reassures the audience that mercy is more appropriate than legal rigor when administered by fallible humanity.

216. Shuger, Debora Kuller. *Political Theologies in Shakespeare's England: The Sacred and the State in "Measure for Measure."* New York: Palgrave, 2001.

Shuger announces that she intends to use *Measure* "as a basis for rethinking English politics and political thought *circa* 1600" (1). Unconcerned with the play's ambiguities and uncertainties, Shuger reads it straightforwardly as a representation of what she terms "high Christian royalism" (31). She believes that Angelo and the Duke represent different channels in late Elizabethan political thought—with Angelo favoring the "good of the community," a concept originating in Plato and espoused most notably by Puritan thinkers, and the Duke believing in the Aristotelian-based "good of the individual," more commonly associated with Anglicanism. Examining the Elizabethan court system, Shuger argues that the ordinary courts dispensed justice according to law, while the equity or prerogative courts—Chancery and Star Chamber—either mitigated laws too harsh or strengthened laws too weak, thus paralleling the approaches Angelo and the Duke take to law. For her, "the Barnardine subplot throws into high relief the issues of penitential justice and the ungodly that are braided into the fabric of the play throughout, and which also lie at the heart of Anglican-Puritan tensions" (124–25). Her short monograph is filled with references to early modern political and theological writers (Martin Bucer, Thomas Edgerton, Richard Hooker, and Niccolo Machiavelli among others), and she concludes that "the Friar-Duke's

Vienna is an attempt to imagine what Christianity might look like as a political praxis" (131).

217. **Spinrad, Phoebe S.** "*Measure for Measure* and the Art of Not Dying." *Texas Studies in Literature and Language* 26 (1984): 74–93. Repr. in Bloom (no. 278).

Considering *Measure* in the context of the Morality tradition, which "poses the moment of death as an understanding of life" (74), Spinrad points out that in *Measure* the resolution death offers is withheld and the problems of life persist. She correlates the characters' attitudes towards death with contemporaneous religious writing. The most prominent image of confinement in the play is the prison. For Spinrad, the Duke's *de contemptu mundi* speech is not unchristian, as some maintain, but, because interrupted, it lacks the requisite appeal for repentance. Isabella's call on her brother for heroism is compared to humanist writings. Isabella, the Duke, and Angelo begin in the mistaken belief that they can order the universe; Angelo's language of "moral regression" (85) parallels a Calvinist delineation of the progress of sin. According to Spinrad, Angelo remains a prisoner of his arbitrary beliefs; the death he twice requests reflects sinful despair, not repentance. The strict restraint Isabella craves in her vocation reflects the language of martyrology and Loyolan meditation; in these terms she imagines her own heroism, a strong contrast to the actual effect her words have on Angelo and to the accommodation she eventually makes. The Duke, controlled by his desire to be loved, acts out a combination of meddlesomeness and passivity that leads him to unhappy truths and to complex exacerbation of problems he could have solved simply. Spinrad concludes that the "falloff which so many audiences have seen" (91) in the second half of *Measure* reflects the "falloff" the characters experience from their imagined ideal worlds into a state in which death is accepted as a part of life, "neither fled from nor sought after" (91).

See also nos. 28, 38, 41, 135, 199, 200, 201, 202, 203, 220, 222, 225, 232, 234, 238, 240, 241, 245, 246a, 249, 251, 253, 258, 259, 260, 263.

D. Language and Linguistics.

218. Empson, William. *The Structure of Complex Words.* 270-88. Ann Arbor: Univ. of Michigan Press, 1951.

Empson chooses the word "sense," which appears ten times in *Measure*, as the basis for investigating doubleness and ambiguity in the play. He suggests that Shakespeare did not like the play's plot and therefore subtly, but consistently, undercut it at critical points. Empson finds most of the characters unlikeable, and reacts strongly against critics who argue that authorial intention cannot be a factor in critical analysis. The argument foreshadows critical debates that would occur twenty years after Empson's essay was published.

See also nos. 137, 223, 229, 237, 257.

E. Criticism.

219. Adelman, Janet. *Suffocating Mothers: Fantasies of Maternal Origin in Shakespeare's Plays, "Hamlet" to "The Tempest,"* 76-102. New York: Routledge, 1992. Repr. in Wheeler (no. 279).

Adelman examines *Measure* and *All's Well* in Chapter 4 of her monograph study of "masculinity and the maternal body in Shakespeare" (2). In her psychological reading of *Measure*, Isabella and all the play's women are confirmed in their necessary sexual roles—though Isabella had desired escape in the convent—by male power which takes over the management of sexuality. Juliet's pregnant body, the origin of the play's action, is displaced by the Duke's machinations only to silently return in the play's final scene. Adelman examines the role of Juliet, or rather of her pregnant body, and of Angelo, deeply split between desire and repression of desire. She reads the Duke as assuming for Isabella the role of an asexual father who will protect her from her own sexuality, and only in the presence of this father can sexuality and marriage be made safe. Whereas Adelman sees the sexuality of *All's Well* in the control of "a sexual woman," she reads *Measure* as putting sexuality under the aegis of "a sternly a-sexual man" (102).

220. Bennett, Josephine Waters. *"Measure for Measure" as Royal Entertainment.* New York: Columbia Univ. Press, 1966.

Bennett argues that *Measure* was selected to open the Christmas Revels at Hampton Court in 1604 because it was suitable for the occasion as a play of "repentance and forgiveness" (8). She reads the play as a comedy throughout, controlled by a clever Duke who teaches important lessons to Angelo and Isabella, "youthful idealists who fail egregiously" (153). Pronouncing the play's ending "delightful in its rightness" (47), Bennett argues that the play alludes to James I's *Basilicon Doron* and is designed to gratify the new monarch. She believes the play was written especially for the occasion, "a showpiece, a special vehicle for exhibition of the skill of both the playwright and the actors" (124). She concludes by speculating on Shakespeare's own skill as an actor, suggesting that he may have played the role of Vincentio.

221. Brown, Carolyn E. "The Wooing of Duke Vincentio and Isabella of *Measure for Measure*: 'The Image of It Gives [Them] Content.'" *Shakespeare Studies* 22 (1994): 189-219.

Starting from Isabella's failure to respond to the Duke's marriage proposal, Brown explores the unusual relationship between these two characters. Noting a persistent unease among critics over their "sexually oriented" involvement in the lives of others, she suggests that they take vicarious pleasure in manipulating their surrogates, Mariana and Angelo. In Brown's psychological reading, Isabella and Vincentio are self-deceived, unaware that their celibacy masks a covert sexuality, revealed in the sexual suggestiveness of their language. Vincentio has more awareness and control, she argues, and manipulates Isabella into shaming herself publicly in order to secure his own public image.

222. Cacicedo, Albert. "'She is fast my wife': Sex, Marriage, and Ducal Authority in *Measure for Measure*." *Shakespeare Studies* 23 (1995): 187-209.

Cacicedo examines the relationship between male authority and "the mother," or licit procreation, as displayed in *Measure*. He believes that the play examines this issue by problematizing the marriage bond; he cites social historians on kinds of marriages, looking at the status of spousals, clandestine marriages, and church-celebrated marriages under civil law, common law, and canon law. He argues that the limits the play puts on sexuality and thus male identity are recuperated in marriage, which erases female identity. The Duke delays his reappearance, Cacicedo argues, to achieve two ends: to show the need for rigorous enforcement of sexual laws and to appear merciful. Similarly, he uses one definition of marriage (spousal) to propel Mariana into Angelo's bed, but insists on another (church-sanctioned) at the play's end to erase any questions about the legitimacy of offspring. All this authoritative manipulation, Cacicedo finds, silences the play's women, tacitly underscoring their dependence upon men.

223. Crane, Mary Thomas. "Male Pregnancy and Cognitive Permeability in *Measure for Measure.*" *Shakespeare Quarterly* 49 (1998): 269-92.

Crane uses cognitive theory to qualify the new historicist assumption that ruling ideologies shape early modern subjects, arguing that the play portrays "the cognitive mechanisms through which the human body and embodied brain both originate and succumb to linguistic expressions of power" (292). Following Shakespeare's use of "pregnant" in *Measure* to refer to male minds enriched with matter, Crane believes that certain characters—Angelo, Isabella, and the Duke—believe themselves impenetrable, sheltered by conscious virtue, convent walls, or a "complete bosom" (282). These fantasies of impermeability are shattered in each case by exposure to language—Isabella's pleas to Angelo, her own confession of sexual shame, and the slanderous attacks of Lucio. Even figures of authority, she asserts, in trying to penetrate and control their subjects are themselves penetrated and changed.

224. Dawson, Anthony B. "*Measure for Measure*, New Historicism and Theatrical Power." *Shakespeare Quarterly* 39 (1988): 328-41.

Dawson begins by critiquing new historicism for ignoring its own ideological basis in contemporary culture, and the political uses to which it puts history. He then turns to *Measure* as an example of the theatrics of power, suggesting that the Duke finds political authority less effective than theatrical manipulation. Focusing on the final scene of *Measure*, Dawson discusses the difference in the way that scene is read by new historicists and the way it is "read" in the theater. Pointing out that both theatrical practice and critical practice are informed by their contemporary cultural context, Dawson nevertheless argues that the theater has more subversive potential than overdetermined new historicist readings which argue that the Duke re-inscribes his hegemonic power and authority in the play's closing scene.

225. Diehl, Huston. " 'Infinite Space': Representation and Reformation in *Measure for Measure.*" *Shakespeare Quarterly* 49 (1998): 393-410.

In opposition to critics who find *Measure* a failed or flawed play, Diehl argues that Shakespeare wished to call attention to the imperfection of his art as part of an examination of the "Protestant aesthetic of the stage" (394). Relating the play to James I's 1604 Hampton Court conference of Puritans and church bishops to attempt a resolution of their differences, Diehl frames the play as a conflict between two extreme views—radical Puritan and Catholic—Angelo's and Isabella's. For Diehl, the play raises metadramatic questions, incorporating the Calvinist view that the physical world is merely a representation: the theater becomes a representation of a representation, communicating only indirect and partial knowledge. Diehl focuses on aspects of the plot—Angelo's lust for Isabella, the bed-trick, and the substitution of the Duke's seal for Angelo's death warrant against Claudio—each dealing with reading a sign correctly or incorrectly. By emphasizing the Duke's own fallibility as a playwright and by the play's imperfect comic ending, Diehl suggests, Shakespeare makes clear that the stage can reveal but not correct imperfection; in a Calvinist framework, perfection and grace come only from the divine.

226. DiGangi, Mario. "Pleasure and Danger: Measuring Female Sexuality in *Measure for Measure*." *ELH* 60 (1993): 589–609. Repr. in Wheeler (no. 279).

In contrast to critics who find *Measure* "impenetrable to feminist criticism" (589), DiGangi asserts that the play may elicit feminist pleasure. Revising the Duke's maid/wife/widow paradigm to one which measures female sexuality: virgin (no partners)/wife (one/legal); whore (more than one/illicit), DiGangi argues that the normative category of wife is unstable. He examines the positions of Juliet, Mariana, and Isabella with regard to their sexuality and then analyzes the scene describing Mistress Elbow (2.1), the play's only wife. Focusing on the scene's suggestive language, DiGangi concludes she may be read as "the wayward wife, who is at once promiscuous ... and opposed to fertility" (592); this wife may, like the virgin, limit her own fertility or, like the whore, open her body to many, both or either of which Mistress Elbow may have been doing in Overdone's establishment. In DiGangi's view, Mistress Elbow's textual presence reminds spectators of the control a wife can exert over her sexual pleasure and fertility, and destabilizes marriage as the bastion of male power.

227. Dodd, William. "Power and Performance: *Measure for Measure* in the Public Theater of 1604–1605." *Shakespeare Studies* 24 (1996): 211–40.

Noting the use of theatrical genre metaphors in public documents from 1603–4, Dodd argues that the difference between tragedy and tragicomedy was well understood by Shakespeare's audience, which would have been aware of the clash between the tragic and comic halves of *Measure*. While the play represents a sovereign staging his power as an attempt to reclaim his authority, Dodd believes that the play actually enacts a loss of authority, due to the consistent undercutting of Vincentio's credibility with the audience. Using the distinction between the *locus* and *platea* stage positions, Dodd argues that Vincentio—disguised, offering asides, planning tricks—should have the *platea* position of engagement with the audience. However, Pompey and Lucio assume this position, undercutting Vincentio and preventing the audience from identifying with the "restoring" Duke. For Dodd, then, the play resists the containment some critics attribute to it and, thanks to the popular tradition in the theater, is open to skeptical political and social interpretation.

228. Dollimore, Jonathan. "Transgression and Surveillance in *Measure for Measure*." In *Political Shakespeare: New Essays in Cultural Materialism*, edited by Jonathan Dollimore and Alan Sinfield, 72–87. Ithaca: Cornell Univ. Press, 1985. Repr. in Wheeler (no. 279).

Against the widely accepted view that sexual anarchy is threatening the social order in *Measure*, Dollimore argues that demonizing illicit sexuality allows authority to assert itself more aggressively. The prostitutes have no presence or voice in the play; only those who wish to exploit them have voices. The Duke provides a fantasy resolution in which law and morality are publicly reconciled, and new constraints are justified as necessary, including the constraints imposed on the submissive women whose marriages the Duke arranges.

229. Eagleton, Terence. *Shakespeare and Society: Critical Studies in Shakespearean Drama*, 66–97. New York: Schocken Books, 1967.

Eagleton's book explores the tension in Shakespearean drama between the self as individual and the self as a responsible member of society. *Measure*, writes Eagleton, deals with the opposition between the law and passion, between the social contract and private emotion. Marriage—which is both deeply personal and a social contract—is an ideal image of this theme. Both the law and language are forms of social communication, and in this play, Eagleton points out, those who abuse language are frequently outsiders, like Lucio, at the margins of society. The Duke ends this play of substitutions by bringing characters together in a form of mutual sharing, in marriage, Eagleton argues, so that the play moves from an initial destructive opposition of law and passion, to fuse them into a positive synthesis, represented by the concluding spate of marriages.

230. Engle, Lars. "*Measure for Measure* and Modernity: The Problem of the Sceptic's Authority." In *Shakespeare and Modernity: Early Modern to Millennium*, edited by Hugh Grady, 85–104. London: Routledge, 2000.

In a volume devoted to considering Shakespeare's relationship to modernism, Engle's essay links Shakespeare and Montaigne (especially in *An Apology for Raymond Sebond*) as pre-modernists who give "undermining satirical descriptions of the meaning-bearing traditions of [their] time" (85). Choosing *Measure* as "a case study of authority issues in a community strongly influenced by Renaissance scepticism" (88), Engle views Vincentio as an uncomfortable sceptic charged with moral leadership. Engle notes that "perspectival thinking" or "competitive re-description" (88) is particularly characteristic of *Measure*, where characters re-describe in various ways not only sex but also religious issues. The Duke has trouble with enforcement, Engle believes, because he wishes "social consultation" or even the consent of the offender to his punishment. When this strategy fails—offenders rarely consent to their own deaths—Vincentio resorts to an uncomfortable universal sentence. For Engle, the play's unsettling ending is thus "the result of a sceptic's failed experiment in the invocation of an absolute" (101).

231. Friedman, Michael D. " 'O, let him marry her!': Matrimony and Recompense in *Measure for Measure*." *Shakespeare Quarterly* 4 (1995): 454–64.

Friedman suggests that the Duke's proposal to Isabella in a "self-imposed form of the same type of recompense he demands of Claudio, Lucio, and Angelo" (454). Though the Duke has not sexually violated her, Friedman points out that he has urged her to publicly slander herself by claiming falsely that Angelo has violated her. After surveying some productions in which a romantic interest was established by subtext or interpolated lines, Friedman asserts that within the play matrimony is a form of recompense for dishonor and suggests a staging of the final scene in which the Duke offers matrimony as recompense for dishonor rather than out of romantic interest.

232. Gless, Darryl J. *"Measure for Measure," the Law, and the Convent.* Princeton: Princeton Univ. Press, 1979.

Gless's monograph offers a reading of *Measure* informed by Christ's Sermon on the Mount (Matthew 5-7), by James I's *Basilicon Doron*, and by an examination of post-Reformation attitudes toward monasticism. His thesis (written to answer critics such as Hawkins [nos. 235 and 236]) is that the Duke, after recognizing his personal frailty and taking responsibility for the corruption in Vienna, "spends the entire play laboring for the good of his subjects" (245). Isabella, Angelo, Lucio, and Claudio are all in need of the Duke's "spiritual physic" (214), Gless argues. He treats Isabella at greatest length, tracing the Duke's step-by-step course of weaning her from "proud religiosity" (83) and her monastic calling. Gless assumes that Isabella accepts the Duke's proposal of marriage, "which confirms her departure from bondage to . . . the world and her entry into a world governed by fruitful married love" (212). Suggesting the allegorical nature of the Duke's portrayal, Gless concludes that his final judgments suggest "the return of divine justice" (254). An appendix deals with the possible influences on the play: Erasmus's colloquy "The Funeral" and the "Isabella Rule" of the London Minoresses, a branch of the Poor Clares.

233. Gurr, Andrew. "*Measure for Measure*'s Hoods and Masks: The Duke, Isabella, and Liberty." *English Literary Renaissance* 27 (1997): 89–105.

Gurr is interested in the hints the text gives about the clothes characters wear and what the clothing may suggest. He argues that Isabella and Vincentio are counterparts from *Measure*'s beginning, both clinging to "the anti-sexual rigor of the absolute law," she by attempting to enter a strict religious order, and he by his "fourteen years of dark and antisocial corners" (93). Isabella is drawn away from her habit of the Poor Clares and, Gurr suggests, must dress as a gentlewoman throughout the play, probably wearing a fashionable black velvet face mask at times. Vincentio falsely assumes the robe and hood of a friar, which he wears until his uncasing by Lucio in Act 5. Gurr believes that their symmetry—including their false identities (Duke as Friar, Isabella as dishonored lady)—hints of the ending Shakespeare would have expected: "the Duke sheds his monkish garb ... Isabella never gets hers on. As half of such a pair of opposites, can she indeed fail to take the Duke's hand when they walk off the stage at the end?" (104).

234. Hall, Jonathan. *Anxious Pleasures: Shakespearean Comedy and the Nation State*, 235–56. Madison, NJ: Fairleigh Dickinson Univ. Press, 1995.

Drawing on Bakhtin, Lacan, Deleuze, and freudian and marxist theorists, Hall reads Shakespearean comedy as representing and implicated in the "schizophrenic" (36) anxieties attendant on the formation of the modern nation state during the sixteenth century. Hall sees *Measure* as opening with the triumph of Lenten values in the state after a period of carnival. Yet the natural cyclicality of this alternation is suspect, he argues, because the cycle is controlled by the Duke rather than occurring naturally. This disruption becomes more disturbing, according to Hall, when it is displaced onto an individual like Angelo, who finds within his Lenten authoritarianism shocking carnivalesque impulses. Though the Duke manipulates plot to a comic resolution, the resolution does not fully satisfy, Hall asserts, because the audience sees the trickery by which the Duke brings about its gratification and is suspicious of absolute power that merely remedies the problems it earlier created.

235. Hawkins, Harriet. *Likenesses of Truth in Elizabethan and Restoration Drama*, 51–78. Oxford: Clarendon Press, 1972.

Hawkins takes as her basic premise that *Measure for Measure* is both "great" and conspicuously flawed (51) most notably because it breaks into two irreconcilable halves. She examines this flaw initially by a comparison with Marston's "successful" (52) *The Malcontent*, a cohesive tragicomedy with stock characters. In contrast, Shakespeare creates unusual absolutist characters clearly intended for tragedy, but whose tragic trajectories are abruptly turned to comedy in the play's second half. Hawkins describes Vincentio's plot interventions: "a previously undistinguished character in a realistic dramatic context suddenly begins, half-way through the action, to exercise prerogatives that are traditionally associated with a dramatic divinity" (62). Noting the power of the characters and the difficulty of their dilemmas in the play's first half, Hawkins bemoans the Duke's actions, "forcing the comic upon the characters and the audience" (69).

236. **Hawkins, Harriet.** " 'The Devil's Party': Virtues and Vices in *Measure for Measure*." *Shakespeare Survey* 31 (1978): 105-13. Repr. in Bloom (no. 278).

Hawkins rejects the proposition that the problems posed in *Measure* can, or should, be solved by recourse to a Renaissance reading of scripture. Asserting the diversity of Renaissance opinion about proper Christian conduct and the intractable complexity of human nature, she finds the problems as they are presented more interesting and important than their solutions. She illustrates this by examining the psychological affinity between Angelo and Isabella, pointing out erotic reciprocity in their speeches which easily inspires conjecture that, had their relationship been consummated, their sensual experience would have been sado-masochistic. The further action of the play leads away from this possibility, but once imagined, she argues, the powerful image persists. Many aspects of the play partake of both virtue and vice: the condemned relationship between Claudio and Juliet, Hawkins points out, is the only mutual love in *Measure*. Thus, for Hawkins, the play's richness lies in the questions for which no answers are provided.

237. **Howard, Jean E.** "*Measure for Measure* and the Restraints of Convention." *Essays in Literature* 10 (1983): 149-58.

Acknowledging the dissonances in character, language, and even genre in *Measure*, Howard argues that these reflect Shakespeare's discontent with the limitations of comic form. Focusing her argument on Vincentio, Howard reads him—especially in the second half of the play—as an artist figure who scripts the actions of those around him, as Prospero later does. This metadramatic reading acknowledges, however, that Vincentio's script is rarely followed. Claudio cannot resign himself to death; Barnardine, Lucio, and Angelo refuse to conform to his plans. Art cannot neatly contain intractable elements of life. The play "deliberately makes problematic its own use of comic conventions and uses the Duke to explore the limitations of a dramaturgy too reliant upon rigid schematization" (155).

238. Ide, Richard S. "Shakespeare's Revisionism: Homiletic Tragicomedy and the Ending of *Measure for Measure.*" *Shakespeare Studies* 20 (1988): 105-27.

Beginning with Jean de Mairet's theory of tragicomedy as presenting a world controlled by Providence where justice is distributed even-handedly, Ide examines late English moralities and Tudor tragicomedies—including *Measure*'s source, Whetstone's *Promos and Cassandra*—as anticipating the Mairet theory. Identifying himself as a "new formalist" who practices "disintegrationist criticism" (107), Ide focuses on the end of *Measure*, where he sees Vincentio, unlike Corvinus in the source, failing to dispense even-handed justice. "Shakespeare initially evokes generic expectations that virtue will be rewarded and vice punished" (111), he writes, but the expectation of justice is undercut by the Duke's response to Isabella's kneeling to beg forgiveness for Angelo. When she knelt earlier for her brother, Angelo was moved by desire, and Ide believes the Duke is similarly moved (his marriage proposal soon follows). Vincentio allows his decisions to be biased by human responses (such as his anger at Lucio's slander). Instead of a neat tragicomic ending, Ide concludes, *Measure* remains open-ended, raising questions about the possibility of earthly justice.

239. Jankowski, Theodora A. *Pure Resistance: Queer Virginity in Early Modern English Drama*, 170-77. Philadelphia: Univ. of Pennsylvania Press, 2000.

In the context of a chapter about "virgin characters who are never recuperated into a patriarchal economy" (171-72), Jankowski considers Isabella as a virgin who is assailed by both Angelo (dishonorably) and the Duke (honorably), neither of whom is content to have her remain a virgin. Her refusal of male power and male sexuality, Jankowski argues, poses a threat to a patriarchal culture that is even greater if Isabella "maintains an erotic life without male contact" because it suggests that a woman could live "with sexual pleasure and without men" (177).

240. Kamps, Ivo. "Ruling Fantasies and the Fantasies of Rule: *The Phoenix* and *Measure for Measure.*" *Studies in Philology* 92 (1995): 248-75.

Looking at *Measure* and Middleton's *The Phoenix* as disguised-ruler plays where the protagonist attempts to reform the society and to re-establish respect for law and authority, Kamps endeavors to explain how a Jacobean audience might have viewed such secretive manipulation by their rulers. Accepting Greenblatt's argument (no. 209) that *Measure* portrays the state "arousing and manipulating anxiety" (249), Kamps suggests that an audience might have welcomed a view of a ruler managing and reforming a society. In a culture which assumed that monarchy was far preferable to democracy, Kamps argues, "a ruler who conducts his affairs by means of guile and deception was not nearly as distasteful ... as it is to us" (257). Kamps rehearses the providential theory of history, in which a ruler acts both as a substitute for God and as a limited human resourcefully attempting to "meet and master an imperfect world" (265). While not denying Greenblatt's argument that the plays portray the management of cultural anxiety, Kamps asserts that they may have also allayed anxiety "about monarchical practices by offering the audience a behind-the-scene look at the 'watchman' at work" (272).

241. Kaplan, M. Lindsay. "Slander for Slander in *Measure for Measure*." *Renaissance Drama* n.s. 21 (1990): 23–54.

Kaplan discusses the function and punishment of slander in Elizabethan England, pointing out that dramatic humiliation was one of the state's weapons in deterring criminal activity and that its use by private citizens was condemned as slander. Thus, Duke Vincentio condemns Lucio's accusations as slander "because Lucio exposes the state's own slanderous practices" (24). These include, according to Kaplan, not only the disguised Duke's public complaints about corruption in Vienna, but also his original act of appointing an ill-equipped substitute whose incompetence opens the government to public criticism. Kaplan says that the Duke's "determination to expose every character on the stage" (45) humiliates and silences his onstage audience and thus "eradicates not only the slander, but also the affirmation of his actions" (45). *Measure*, she argues, warns "that the greatest peril of theatrical slander lies in the ruler's, not the theater's, use of it" (47).

242. Kirsch, Arthur. *Shakespeare and the Experience of Love*, 71–107. Cambridge: Cambridge Univ. Press, 1981.

Kirsch reads the play as a tragicomedy, an explication of the Christian experience, which moves from impending death to impending marriage, and from sin to grace. Reacting against a 1974 production in which Isabella drew back in horror from the Duke's offer of marriage, Kirsch sees both Isabella and Angelo as at fault, in need of the testing and instruction that the Duke proceeds to give them. Thus the play exemplifies the idea of *felix culpa*, and the Duke assumes a truly godlike role.

243. **Kliman, Bernice W.** "Isabella in *Measure for Measure*." *Shakespeare Studies* 15 (1982): 137–48.

Kliman argues that, despite her brother's claim otherwise, Isabella is a weak and illogical rhetorician who fails to follow the well-known rules for rhetoric laid down by Aristotle and Cicero. According to Kliman, Shakespeare deliberately weakens Isabella in comparison to his sources' heroines in order to "deflect the audience's attention from her and focus on ... the Duke" (139) and his justice. She believes that this interpretation would be rich and complex in performance.

244. **Knight, G. Wilson.** *The Wheel of Fire: Interpretation of Shakespeare's Tragedy*, 80–106. Oxford: Oxford Univ. Press, 1930.

Declaring that the ethics of *Measure* are those of the Christian gospels, Knight offers a somewhat allegorical reading. For him, the Duke is the patriarchal center of the play; his "sense of human responsibility is delightful throughout: he is like a kindly father, and all the rest are his children" (79). Angelo is "ensnared by good, by his own love of sanctity, exquisitely symbolized in his love of Isabella" (88–89), he writes, and Isabella is lacking in human feeling. Knight attributes the Duke's leniency in Act 5 to his new understanding of the complex nature of men. He believes that the Duke follows the ethical teachings of Jesus and that the play should be read like a parable, reflecting "the sublime strangeness and unreason of Jesus's teaching" (96).

245. **Knoppers, Laura Lungers.** "(En)gendering Shame: *Measure for Measure* and the Spectacles of Power." *English Literary Renaissance* 23 (1993): 450–71.

Knoppers addresses the conflict between new historicist critics and feminist critics over *Measure*; her reading attends, she asserts, to both political power and gender. Discussing the shaming rituals meted out by both Church and State for sexual offenses, Knoppers finds that the Church shamed both men and women in an effort to reform behavior while the State focused on deterrence, rather than reform, by shaming women with rituals that were excessive and voyeuristic for spectators. Knoppers reads Isabella's repeated kneeling in the play's final scene—to confess fornication and to pray for her brother's murderer—as a form of shaming. To shame Angelo politically, Knoppers argues, women themselves must be sexually shamed, as is Lucio's prostitute, who is never onstage but is repeatedly referred to in degrading terms. Knoppers believes that by keeping silent after being exposed to the Duke's gaze and offer of marriage, Isabella "blocks closure in the ending of *Measure* and exposes the play's complicity in the (en)gendering of shame it professes to interrogate" (471).

246. Lamb, Mary Ellen. "Shakespeare's 'Theatrics': Ambivalence toward Theater in *Measure for Measure.*" *Shakespeare Studies* 20 (1988): 129–46.

Lamb argues that divergent readings of *Measure*—as an optimistic play about the restoration of order to a society, or as a dark satire about a society that cannot reform—depend on contrasting interpretations of the character of the Duke and, indeed, of the theater itself. Pairing the Duke and Lucio, Lamb examines them as stage managers who tell other characters what roles to play. In some cases, Lamb asserts, role-playing seems positive, as when it liberates Isabella from her "initial rigidity' (134) as a novice. But when Lucio—and perhaps the Duke—seems to lose sight of the difference "between theater and life" (140), role-playing becomes less attractive. Concluding that the play withholds the information necessary for a decisive interpretation of the Duke or the theater, Lamb nevertheless celebrates *Measure*'s gaps, which force the audience to construct its own interpretations.

246a. Lascelles, Mary. *Shakespeare's "Measure for Measure."* London: Athlone Press, 1953.

Lascelles begins her leisurely look at *Measure* by examining the plot, which she terms "the monstrous ransom" (7). She looks at source stories and analogues, most particularly Cinthio's *Hecatomithi* and Whetstone's *Promos and Cassandra* as well as the adaptations of *Measure* by Davenant (see no. 271) and Gildon (see no. 272). She examines the Folio text, offering explanations of troubling passages or stage directions. Generally, this early study accepts *Measure* as a "great, uneven play" (164), a tragicomedy, and argues against readings which claim parts are not Shakespeare's or which allegorize the characters and plot.

247. Leavis, F. R. *The Common Pursuit*, 160–72. London: Chatto and Windus, 1952.

Reacting to L. C. Knight's *Scrutiny* essay (10:3) on *Measure*, Leavis offers an opposing view. To him, *Measure* is not a problem play. He believes the Duke—who is Shakespeare's addition to the source story—voices the reader's/audience's point of view. Leavis sees the play's plot as a complex experiment controlled by the Duke. He finds the play's ending satisfying, "marvelously adroit, with an adroitness that expresses, and derives from, the poet's sure human insights and his firmness of ethical and poetic sensibility" (169). Leavis refuses to label characters like Angelo and Isabella as evil or good. Both are flawed, he argues, but not without their virtues. And both are brought by the Duke's experiment, Leavis believes, to greater self-awareness and humanity.

248. Leggatt, Alexander. "Substitution in *Measure for Measure.*" *Shakespeare Quarterly* 39 (1988): 342-59.

Noting, as have other critics (see nos. 240, 241, 260), the prevalence of substitution in *Measure*—Mariana for Isabella, Angelo for the Duke, Barnardine for Claudio—Leggatt examines the problems of the various exchanges. He argues that political exchange is made to look futile, as is the bed-trick exchange. The substitutes are alike, but also different, he writes, for eventually all the equations between characters break down, as do the substitutions that critics have suggested reach outside the play—the Duke for King James, or the Duke for the playwright. Leggatt believes that Shakespeare struggled with *Measure*, and in so doing created substitutions that are revealing but incomplete.

249. Levin, Richard. *New Readings vs. Old Plays: Recent Trends in the Reinterpretation of English Renaissance Drama*, 171-93. Chicago: Univ. of Chicago Press, 1979; pb. 1982.

Levin's book is devoted to attacking three critical approaches to Renaissance drama which have produced multiple "readings." His concluding section, on *Measure*, deals with the new historicist approach, which, Levin says, uses some bit of extra-dramatic background to determine the "real" meaning of a play. Quoting extensively from critics who have compared *Measure* to James I's *Basilicon Doron*, Levin argues that the similarities are mostly commonplaces, and that some seem opposite to what James advocated. He continues by debunking the other topical references that critics ordinarily cite as proof that the play was written specifically for presentation before James. He concludes by asking what we would learn about such a piece of dramatic art if topicality could be proved.

250. Little, Arthur L., Jr. "Absolute Bodies, Absolute Laws: Staging Punishment in *Measure for Measure.*" In *Shakespearean Power and Punishment*, edited by Gillian Murray Kendall, 113-29. Madison, NJ: Fairleigh Dickinson Univ. Press, 1998.

Drawing upon Foucault's discussions of the punitive body and Bakhtin's distinction between the classical and the grotesque body, Little argues that the Duke "uses his power of punishment in order to assure his subjects of their non-absolute or unfinished status ... of the inability of their bodies to survive without him" (115). Little also emphasizes the relationship between the Duke's "staging of his political theater" and "the politics of Shakespeare's staging of an absolutist ruler" (115). He comments on the apparently "finished" bodies of the "enskied" Isabella and of Angelo, "one who never feels" (119), as competitive with the Duke's own classical body. The Duke reduces these bodies, and all others in the play, to their grotesque form in "a Foucauldian ritual of public punishment" (119). In Act 5, the Duke overrules the absolutist laws he never enforced in a display of his own absolute power, according to Little. His public return, staged in what Little terms "the marketplace" (123) where grotesque bodies and rampant speech are to be found, dramatically reveals his control over all of Vienna. Finally, Little argues, such visions of absolute rule—whether by Vincentio or by James I—are self-deluding: "there is a power more absolute than the ruler, and that is the power to stage him" (126).

251. Miles, Rosalind. *The Problem of "Measure for Measure."* New York: Barnes & Noble, 1976.

Miles first surveys eighteenth- and nineteenth-century attitudes toward the success of *Measure* and its characters, continuing in Chapters 2 and 3 to look at twentieth-century criticism, where judgment frequently changes from the "failure" of earlier centuries to "problem." Her purpose, after noting the conflicting criticism, is to "attempt a full objective assessment of the position of *Measure*" (94). In a chapter entitled "Practical Criticism," Miles discusses revisions and performance versions of the play including Davenant's revision, the illustrations of various *Measure* editions in the eighteenth and nineteenth centuries, and, briefly, paintings the play inspired. After examining the "disguised duke" plays of Marston and Middleton (where the stock figure is used for irony and satire), disguise in Shakespeare's drama, and the treatment of the friar character in the period, Miles considers *Measure*'s Duke as the product of these traditions. Miles goes on to consider Angelo and Isabella as tested and given a "spiritual education" (229) by the Duke. She looks at the play's structure, including plot mechanisms such as the bed-trick and the obligatory happy ending, and concludes that the play is only partially successful. Five appendices complete the volume: a collection of some "extreme views" of the play; a chart showing the distribution of *Measure*'s lines among the three principal characters; twentieth-century examples of what Miles calls the "corrupt bargain"; a brief stage history; and costume lists for London productions in 1816 and 1824.

252. Paster, Gail Kern. *The Idea of the City in the Age of Shakespeare,* 205–19. Athens, GA: Univ. of Georgia Press, 1985.

Paster suggests that narrative discontinuity in *Measure* introduces the social discontinuity of life in a city, evidenced in the play by lack of family and domestic life. This environment, Paster argues, produces narcissists, characters full of self-regard. Substitution in *Measure*, according to Paster, is a way for characters to look at themselves, as Vincentio does in appointing Angelo. Isabella's self-love is focused on her chastity, while Angelo's desire for her is for someone like himself. Seeing the prison as a microcosm of the city, Paster argues that only the theater can contain the prison, so that the Duke stages his return before an audience and thereby releases himself, Isabella, and perhaps Angelo from their fixation on self. But she cautions that the theatrical image also suggests that this new community formed through marriages may be only illusion.

253. Pendleton, Thomas A. "Shakespeare's Disguised Duke Play: Middleton, Marston, and the Sources of *Measure for Measure.*" In *"Fanned and Winnowed Opinions": Shakespearean Essays Presented to Harold Jenkins,* edited by John W. Mahon and Thomas A. Pendleton, 79–97. London: Methuen, 1987.

Pendleton argues that Duke Vincentio derives from the disguised rulers found in Middleton's *The Phoenix* and Marston's *The Malcontent,* who also disguise to observe, expose, and ultimately thwart the vices and follies of their realms. After arguing that the dates of Marston and Middleton's plays place them before *Measure* (1604), Pendleton enumerates the plot parallels and verbal similarities of the plays. He concludes, however, that Vincentio's characterization remains a problem in *Measure,* calling him a "failed stage duke."

254. Price, Jonathan R. "*Measure for Measure* and the Critics: Towards a New Approach." *Shakespeare Quarterly* 20 (1969): 179–204.

Price surveys in broad terms critical approaches to *Measure,* including the eighteenth-century focus on the situations the play presents, the romantic critics' interest in Shakespeare the artist, late nineteenth-century analysis of the play's characters, and the twentieth century's interest in the play's "meaning." Separating strands of twentieth-century critical concern, Price treats in greater detail critics who search for unity, those who search for ethical Christianity, those who are concerned about genre, and finally those who are fascinated by the ambiguity of the play and the inconsistencies of its characters. It is with these latter critics that he casts his own lot, concluding that Shakespeare was deliberately ambiguous and inconsistent in order to interest his audience, to draw them into hard thinking about *Measure*.

255. **Riefer, Marcia.** " 'Instruments of Some More Mightier Member': The Construction of Female Power in *Measure for Measure*." *Shakespeare Quarterly* 35 (1984): 157-69. Repr. in Bloom (no. 278).

This essay traces Isabella's transformation and loss of autonomy, as she changes from an articulate, self-determined woman to an obedient follower of male direction, an actress in a male-authored drama. Riefer locates this transformation in the power of the patriarchal structures in the play—Vincentio represents both Church and State—and argues that the play explores the incompatibility of patriarchal and comic structures. She also views Vincentio as a "third-rate playwright," arguing that the action that he scripts is designed to display himself to advantage with little regard for what he does to others. Despite his effectiveness in controlling the play's women, however, Riefer notes that some of the male characters—Barnardine, Lucio, and Claudio—refuse to completely submit to his script.

256. **Rossiter, A. P.** "*Measure for Measure*." In *Angel with Horns: Fifteen Lectures on Shakespeare*, edited by Graham Storey, 152-70. London: Longmans, Green & Co., 1961. Repr. in Bloom (no. 278).

For Rossiter the enduring value of *Measure* lies in its "keen and insightful inquisition into man's nature" (170) rather than in the Christian interpretations offered by many of his contemporary critics. He reads the play as an interrogation of the adequacy of law to regulate matters of instinct played out in a tragicomic genre that manipulates empirical observations rather than *a priori* hypotheses. For him, the play images the "world-upside-down" topos. The disorder and corruption unleashed by the Duke's abrogation reveal Claudio and Isabella to be alike, and very human, in their conflicted but urgent desire for self-preservation. Ambiguity in the characters, situations, and language marks the life-like complexity of the problem-setting in the first three acts, Rossiter asserts, choosing only Barnardine and the Duke's "Be absolute for death" speech (3.1) as admirably unambiguous. Disagreeing specifically with Knight (no. 244) and Leavis (no. 247), he finds that the solution imposed in the last two acts lacks the character development or finely textured writing needed to achieve the ending in Christian ethics that Shakespeare intended.

257. **Schleiner, Louise.** "Providential Improvisation in *Measure for Measure*." *PMLA* 97 (1982): 227-36. Repr. in Bloom (no. 278).

Noting that twentieth-century interpretations of the Duke's pivotal role have swung between extremes of moralistic aversion and deification, Schleiner argues that the central paradigm of the play is derived from the absentee-master who tests his servants, found in several New Testament parables and employed in *Measure* ironically. The Duke is a flawed, but well-intentioned, ruler attempting with comic results to imitate God, she argues, and his efforts to act as moral tester and teacher are repeatedly challenged throughout the play by the force of "natural human drives" and "thus the theological pattern works dialectically" (232). For Schleiner, the insistent and, at times, attractive voice of human evil undermines the divinity of the Duke, making the very real humor of the play a black humor, "reinforcing themes of hollow justice and tyrannous authority" (231). Schleiner sees subtle allusions to the quickly mounting evidence that James would not live up to the ideas expressed in his *Basilicon Doron* and other ironic moments which could not have been stressed at court but which are often integral to modern productions. Nevertheless, she sees the Duke as a well-intentioned, if quixotic, figure who attempts to govern well, but whose plans are inevitably interrupted and distorted.

258. **Shell, Marc.** *The End of Kinship: "Measure for Measure," Incest, and the Ideal of Universal Siblinghood.* Stanford: Stanford Univ. Press, 1988; repr. Baltimore: The Johns Hopkins Univ. Press, 1995.

For a study of the concept of universal siblinghood and its effect on political and economic hierarchy, Shell minutely examines the relationships, both civil and religious, of *Measure*. Noting the identity of Isabella as both biological sister to Claudio and as spiritual Sister in the order of Clares, and Vincentio's double role as patriarchal father to Vienna as well as Father Friar and Brother Friar, Shell considers bastardy, incest, *lex talionis* (eye for an eye, or measure for measure), and familial relationships in civic and religious contexts. Taking as his central theme Isabella's rhetorical question to Claudio: "Is't not a kind of incest, to take life/ From thine own sister's shame?" (3.1.38-39), Shell draws from sixteenth-century philosophy and history to contextualize this theme in *Measure*. The use to which his study puts the play is exemplified by a quotation from his conclusion: "*Measure for Measure* suggests the fictional, or dreamlike, quality of marriage. ... because what marriage purports to accomplish—a chaste solution to the confrontation between civilization (the rule against incest) and nature (the rule to reproduce no matter how)—it accomplishes only by violation of the incest taboo" (177).

259. **Stevenson, David Lloyd.** *The Achievement of Shakespeare's "Measure for Measure."* Ithaca: Cornell Univ. Press, 1966.

In his slim monograph, Stevenson attacks the assumption that *Measure* is a problem play. He argues, following Leavis (no. 247), that "it is a brilliant, self-contained artistic achievement. . . . an intellectual comedy" (5). He finds the structure of the play carefully balanced and provides a scene-by-scene commentary, followed by a discussion of critical responses from the eighteenth century to the mid-twentieth century, always arguing against those who have found the play flawed. Particularly opposed to the critics who read the play as moral or theological allegory (chiefly Battenhouse, see no. 204), Stevenson devotes a chapter to challenging their Christianized readings. After a brief conclusion summarizing the virtues of this "idiosyncratic" (123), "uncomfortable" (131) play, Stevenson ends the volume with an appendix arguing that Shakespeare wrote *Measure* with the newly-crowned King James I in mind, including in it the concern with justice and mercy which James had just expressed in *Basilicon Doron*.

260. **Tennenhouse, Leonard.** "Representing Power: *Measure for Measure* in its Time." In *The Forms of Power and the Power of Forms in the Renaissance*, edited by Stephen Greenblatt. *Genre* 15 (1982): 139-56.

Tennenhouse considers *Measure* as part of a group of disguised ruler plays written about 1604-1606 and suggests that they are central to a genre shift in drama occurring about this time. These plays present a state run by substitutes separate from the monarch, he argues, and prefigure the later concept of state as bureaucracy. However, since these bureaucracies are flawed and must be taken in hand by the disguised ruler, the plays suggest, according to Tennenhouse, that only the true monarch can make the state function properly. Pointing out that the disguised figure's purpose is to protect marriage and regulate desire, Tennenhouse examines the contrasting behavior of Elizabeth and James with regard to the marriages of their courtiers and concludes that James, positioning himself as generous father and philosopher king, was trying to restore the monarchy to a patriarchy, like the disguised ruler replacing his substitute.

261. **Watson, Robert N.** "False Immortality in *Measure for Measure*: Comic Means, Tragic Ends." *Shakespeare Quarterly* 41 (1990): 411-32.

After asserting that *Measure* is a tragicomedy, Watson examines the tension that he finds in the play between the need for lawful procreation and the examination of individual life as terminal and bereft of illusions of immortality. *Measure*'s comic message, for Watson, appears when the race's extinction, either by asceticism or by libertinism, is avoided in a resolution of marriage. Its tragic message he finds much more intricately explored in the systemic rejection of hopes for individual immortality. Individual desire and difference (as in Isabella's convent vocation) Watson sees as erased by the state's need for sanctioned procreation.

262. Weil, Herbert, Jr. "Form and Contexts in *Measure for Measure.*" *Critical Quarterly* 12 (1970): 55–72. Repr. in Bloom (no. 278).

Weil maintains that the often-noted falling off of dramatic intensity in the second half of *Measure* is essential to an authorial design that purposefully mingles the comic, the serious, and the problematic. Thus, most of the descending action should be interpreted in "a light comic, often farcical, vein" (55). Shakespeare prepares for the dramatic shift which occurs when the Duke interrupts Isabella's condemnation of her brother (3.1.152), according to Weil, through the use of the comic subplot for exposition and in the rhythmic alternation of idealistic statements and low humor. The remainder of the play is dominated by the Duke and the low-life characters whose interactions reveal that the Duke is well-intentioned, but deeply flawed and self-deceived. The shift in focus away from a serious treatment of the moral problems emphatically posed in the first two acts is mirrored in the structure of the fifth act, Weil believes, and the inadequate comic ending deliberately leaves the crucial thematic problems of the play unresolved, as it reveals the limits and expands the potential of comic conventions.

263. Yachnin, Paul. "The Politics of Theatrical Mirth: *A Midsummer Night's Dream, A Mad World, My Masters*, and *Measure for Measure.*" *Shakespeare Quarterly* 43 (1992): 51–66.

In what he terms an "historicized metadramatic reading of *Measure*," Yachnin contrasts the play with the two other plays in his title. Seeing all three caught between the competing visions of a theater supported either by commercialism or by patronage, he reads *A Midsummer Night's Dream* as containing the competition within a vision of community, mediated by mirth, in which tradesmen and courtiers are largely ignorant of each other's view of theater. In Middleton's *A Mad World, My Masters*, he asserts, theater is represented as the product of self-interest; theatrical mirth is counterfeit and wholly commercial. By contrast in *Measure*, Yachnin argues, Shakespeare does not defend theater in public terms (representing social harmony) but defends it on private grounds (converting individuals). *Measure* is resolved, for Yachnin, only in the private renewal of some characters. In this shift from public to private, Yachnin finds Shakespeare's definition of mirth narrowed, eroticized, and demonized in order to provide exempla of conversion. For Yachnin, this attempt to legitimize the theater on private grounds remains unsatisfying because of uncertainty about the private self: is Vincentio a "sovereign evangelist" or a "scheming confidence-man"? (65).

See also nos. 141, 145, 149, 165, 181, 201, 202, 205.

F. Stage History; Productions; Performance Criticism; Film and Television Versions.

264. McGuire, Philip C. *Speechless Dialect: Shakespeare's Open Silences*, 63–96. Berkeley: Univ. of California Press, 1985.

McGuire's monograph is concerned with Shakespearean open silences "whose precise meaning and effects ... must be established by nonverbal, extra-textual features of the play that emerge only in performance" (xv). In Chapter 4, he examines the final scene of *Measure* and the six open silences he finds therein: Barnardine's after his pardon; Angelo's toward Mariana; Claudio's toward both Juliet and Isabella; Isabella's toward both Claudio and the Duke. To show how performance choices alter the meanings these silences can convey, McGuire looks at five productions: Keith Hack's (RSC, 1974), Desmond Davis's (BBC TV, 1979), Barry Kyle's (RSC, 1978), Robin Phillips's (Stratford, Ont., 1975), and David Giles's (Stratford, Ont., 1969). He concludes, "The open silences that abound during [*Measure's*] final moments ensure that its generic identity is not fixed and cannot be definitely specified" (96).

265. *Measure for Measure*. London: British Broadcasting Corporation, 1979.

This script for the 1979 BBC TV production of *Measure*, based on the edition edited by Peter Alexander, notes textual cuts in the margins. In addition to the script itself, the volume includes a "Preface" by Cedric Messina, an essay "The Production" by Henry Fenwick, a note on the text by Alan Shallcross, "the BBC TV Cast and Production Team," color and black-and-white photographs of the production, and a glossary of difficult words or unfamiliar usages cross-referenced to their appearance in the script. Most notable is Fenwick's essay on the production, which discusses the particular choices made by the producer, director (Desmond Davis), designer, and some of the actors to ready this play for television. Clearly influenced in many ways by Bennett's study of *Measure* (no. 220), Davis nonetheless sees the great confrontation of the play as that between Isabella (Kate Nelligan) and Angelo (Tim Pigott-Smith), newly powerful as the Duke's substitute.

265a. Moore, Don D. "Three Stage Versions of *Measure for Measure*'s Duke: The Providential, the Pathetic, the Personable." *Explorations in Renaissance Culture* 12 (1986): 58–67.

Acknowledging the critical debate fought over decades about the character of Duke Vincentio, Moore examines three productions for their realizations of the character. The Old Vic Company's 1963 production, directed by Michael Elliot, featured a Duke who was almost Christ-like. This production, Moore says, was dominated by the Duke's saintly presence. In contrast, John Barton's 1970 production at Stratford offered a tentative, uncertain Duke, completely out of his element in a world focused instead on "the icy brilliance of ... Angelo" (61). The third example was Adrian Noble's 1983 Stratford production. The Duke, according to Moore, was "personable and human" (63). Moore calls this last "the most fully realized Duke in the most acclaimed production ... in recent years" (64). His point is that productions imitate, and sometimes lead, readings produced in the scholarly study.

266. Rocklin, Edward L. "Measured Endings: How Productions Close Shakespeare's Open Silences in *Measure for Measure.*" *Shakespeare Survey* 53 (2000): 213–32.

Using McGuire's definition of "open silences" (no. 264), Rocklin explores how productions of *Measure*, beginning with a Theatre Royal production in 1722, have dealt with two of the play's open silences: Isabella's when the Duke proposes and the silence between Claudio and Isabella, begun in 3.1 and continued in 5.1. Noting that a performance text often influences the next production, Rocklin finds that in the eighteenth century the Duke's lines at the end of Act 5 were regularly rewritten in order to create a single, but more fulsome, proposal. In nineteenth- and early twentieth-century productions, Claudio either asked Isabella's pardon in 3.1 or was given reconciliatory stage business. Likewise in Act 5, Isabella and Claudio often embraced to signal their happy reunion. All these changes supported the play as comedy, Rocklin argues. Only in productions beginning around 1970, he asserts, have the silences remained open, suggesting tragicomedy or a play that refuses "the image of harmony" (232).

267. Scott, Michael. *Renaissance Drama and a Modern Audience*, 61–75. London: Macmillan, 1982.

Scott surveys seven British productions of *Measure* from the 1970s: three from the RSC (Barton, 1970; Hack, 1974; Kyle, 1978–79); Burge's at the Edinburgh Festival in 1976; Gill's for Riverside Studios in 1979; the 1979 BBC production; and Marowitz's 1975 adaptation at the Open Space. The features of the productions which Scott discusses include the portrayals of particular characters (the Duke, Isabella, Angelo, and Barnardine), the stagings of the marriage proposal, and the sets. Noting the popularity of the play with directors in the 1970s, Scott speculates that "in its emphasis on the bankruptcy of law and order, and in its exposure of the impotence of both lax and over-rigid governmental controls, it may have also appealed to a society attempting to regain its economic and political stability" (75).

268. Weil, Herbert, Jr. "The Options of the Audience: Theory and Practice in Peter Brook's *Measure for Measure.*" *Shakespeare Survey* 25 (1972): 25-35.

Weil is interested in ways theater productions and literary scholarship do or do not complement each other. As his example, he looks at Brook's 1950 production at Stratford-upon-Avon, comparing the promptbook for that production with Brook's discussion of the play in *The Empty Space* (1968). Applauding Brook's analysis of the play as showing the coexistence of "the Holy and the Rough," Weil examines the production promptbook to discover how this contrast was realized. Weil notes with disappointment that, in the interest of staging an admirable Duke, "an ideal ruler," Brook cut lines which show the Duke in an unflattering light. Weil discusses these missing lines and concludes that the "brilliant modern interpretation" Brook suggests in his book was not staged in his 1950 production.

269. Williamson, Jane. "The Duke and Isabella on the Modern Stage." In *The Triple Bond: Plays, Mainly Shakespearean, in Performance*, edited by Joseph G. Price and Helen D. Willard, 149-69. University Park: Pennsylvania State Univ. Press, 1975.

Williamson describes the ways Duke Vincentio and Isabella were played in a score of professional productions from 1950 (Peter Brook's at Stratford-upon-Avon) to 1970 (John Barton's at Stratford-upon-Avon). She finds that the Dukes of the 1950s were generally authoritative and benevolent "royal princes" (169) who advised young, innocent Isabellas. By contrast, the Dukes of the 1960s were "godlike" (163), taking on more than human authority and guiding Isabellas who ranged from secular, to taut and passionate, to complex and contradictory. In the final two productions she discusses—Stratford, Ontario, 1969, and Stratford-upon-Avon, 1970—Williamson finds that the Dukes "returned to human dimensions" (165). In fact, in the 1970 production, a "feminist" Isabella (165) refused the Duke's offer of marriage, underscoring his characterization as "a genial bumbler" (169).

See also nos. 28, 30, 35, 36, 199, 200, 201, 224, 231, 233, 242, 243, 251, 277.

G. Adaptations.

270. Brecht, Bertolt. "Roundheads and Peakheads." In *Jungle of Cities and Other Plays*, edited by Eric Bentley, 163-280. New York: Grove Press, 1966.

Titled in the first draft by Brecht "Measure for Measure of The Salt Tax," this play takes place in Yahoo, where the Regent finds himself in terrible financial trouble because of disputes between landowners and their impoverished tenants. Calling in Iberin to rule in his place, the Regent departs, and Iberin sets up a new government which supports all citizens with round heads and persecutes those with peaked heads. This strategy divides both landowning and tenant classes and eventually results in the suppression of the Sicklemen, a group of militant tenants. In the meantime, a peakheaded landowner is arrested for seducing the daughter of his roundheaded tenant and condemned to death. His sister, Isabella, who has just arranged to enter a convent, learns that she can save her brother if she gives herself to Iberin's second-in-command. The tenant's daughter, a prostitute, is persuaded by the brothel owner to substitute for Isabella at the assignation. The Regent returns, declaring that Roundheads and Peakheads must work together to defeat their common enemies in the neighboring country, and all ends much the same as it was at the play's beginning, except that a freshly-painted sickle is revealed as the play closes. The play (written in 1931-32) in part satirizes the rise of Nazism and Hitler.

271. Davenant, Sir William. *The Law Against Lovers*. In *Measure for Measure: The Bankside Restoration Shakespeare*, edited by Appleton Morgan. New York: Shakespeare Press, 1908.

This edition prints the folio text of *Measure* opposite Davenant's text of *The Law Against Lovers* (performed 1662, printed 1673). Davenant's play combines the Beatrice and Benedick plot from *Much Ado About Nothing* with *Measure*, from which Davenant omits Mariana and the subplot characters except Pompey, whom he turns into a Fool. Set in Turin, the play records the Duke's decision to invest Angelo with his power. Angelo's brother, Benedick, returns from a successful military campaign to be met by a scornful Beatrice (a wealthy heiress who is Angelo's ward). Claudio and Juliet are imprisoned for breaking the law against fornication, and Isabel is summoned from the convent to plead for her brother. Angelo offers her the sexual bargain, which she refuses; Claudio, hearing of her refusal, says she did the right thing. Juliet, however, reproaches her for refusing until Isabel suggests that Juliet take her place in Angelo's bed, and Juliet realizes she can't. Benedick and Beatrice plot to free Claudio and Juliet, while remaining scornful of marriage and each other, and

Claudio and Juliet each scheme separately to rescue the other through self-sacrifice, while Angelo reveals to Isabel that Claudio's arrest was merely a ploy to remove her from the convent and test her virtue. Isabel rejects his offer of marriage. Before Angelo can release Claudio, Benedick mounts a successful mutiny to rescue Claudio and Juliet, and the Duke re-emerges to order the Provost to open the prison gates and release the prisoners. No marriages take place or are promised. The play includes several songs, including one beginning "Our Ruler has got the vertigo of State" (157). For a facsimile of the 1673 text, see no. 272.

272. Gildon, Charles. *Measure for Measure, or Beauty the Best Advocate,* edited by Edward A. Cairns. New York: Garland, 1987.

Gildon's commercially successful 1700 adaptation of *Measure* incorporated some of Davenant's *The Law Against Lovers* (no. 271). Gildon added musical entertainments derived from Henry Purcell's 1680 opera, *Dido and Aeneas*, with libretto by Nahum Tate, and attempted to "improve" the plot in line with neo-classical principles while retaining Shakespeare's unique "witchery" (25). The largest part of stage time was given to music and dance designed to reform Angelo. "Music," Cairns writes, "expresses natural order and geauty [sic] for Gildon and reinforces the fact that Isabella too is represented as the ultimate combination of order and beauty, which is the best advocate" (59). Rapid pace, plot unity, simplification of character, and decorum are achieved, primarily by eliminating the low-life plot and making Angelo aware that Claudio and Julietta are formally, though clandestinely, married. Gildon retains Davenant's introduction of an attempt by Angelo to purchase Isabella's sexual compliance with jewels, but he does not follow Davenant in providing the Deputy with possible exculpatory proposals of marriage. Reduction in the complexity of the roles of Isabella and the Duke de-emphasizes themes related to governance and religion. Cairns provides a chronology of Gildon's life and examines Gildon's play in comparison with Shakespeare's *Measure* and Davenant's adaptation. A brief textual introduction states that the single printed text, the 1700 Quarto, has been supplemented by conflation with a modern collation of existing manuscripts of the opera and libretto. Textual notes and commentary appear at the foot of each page of this old-spelling edition. A facsimile of the 1673 folio text of *The Law Against Lovers* is printed in an appendix.

273. Marowitz, Charles. *The Marowitz Shakespeare: Adaptations and Collages of "Hamlet," "Macbeth," "The Taming of the Shrew," "Measure for Measure," and the "Merchant of Venice,"* 181–225. New York: Drama Book Specialists, 1978.

Marowitz adapts Shakespeare's *Measure* to his own purposes in the spirit of Artaud's "exhortation to destroy masterpieces" (18). The adaptation essentially follows Shakespeare's main plot and language until, in the absence of the Duke's guiding presence, Isabella succumbs to Angelo and Claudio is, nevertheless, executed. The Duke sentences Isabella to prison, and the play ends with the authority figures raucously disporting themselves in the language of the low-life sub-plot of Shakespeare's play. Marowitz provides strongly interpretive stage directions, and in his introduction he identifies the purpose of his *Measure* as an attempt to arouse the audience to anger with "the workings of society—particularly that branch which calls itself the Law. ... the deadly mechanism by which favours and prejudice are allowed to trample innocence and dissent" (21).

274. **Slavitt, David R.** "Luke's Book." In *Get Thee to a Nunnery: A Pair of Shakespeare Divertimentos*, 9–73. North Haven, CT: Catbird Press, 1999.

In a short story set in the old territory of New Mexico and recounted by an intellectually introspective Luke (counterpart to Lucio), Slavitt retells *Measure* as a sordid modern fable reflecting on self-delusion and social manipulation.

H. Pedagogy.

275. **Gibson, Rex, and Jane Coles,** eds. *Measure for Measure.* Cambridge School Shakespeare. Cambridge: Cambridge Univ. Press, 1993.

This instructional edition prints the full text of the New Cambridge Shakespeare *Measure* (no. 201). Facing each page of text are summaries, annotations, and many suggestions for individual and group learning activities. These range from simple questions to speculative and research writing assignments, improvisational acting suggestions, and debate, directing, and classroom performance exercises. Illustrations, especially performance photos, are used primarily to encourage students to consider the variety and techniques of interpretation. Additional activities are suggested at the end of each act. The volume concludes with more ideas and activities organized around topics such as the writer, justice and mercy, sex and sexuality.

276. **Hamilton, A. C.** "On Teaching the Shakespeare Canon: The Case of *Measure for Measure*." In *Teaching Shakespeare*, edited by Walter Edens et al., 95–113. Princeton: Princeton Univ. Press, 1977.

Hamilton suggests that "the neglected art of teaching" can offer a much-needed guide for furiously proliferating criticism (95). Experience with a variety of methods in teaching Shakespeare to university students left Hamilton dissatisfied, but touring with a company that was performing *Measure* and speaking with the audiences in small towns was a turning point for him. The discussions, especially the frequent hostility of these audiences to Isabella's determined chastity and the Duke's manipulations, convinced Hamilton that characters should not be judged outside the context of the play. He concludes that study of *Measure*, with its movement from tragic resolves to comic resolutions, requires the consideration of the entire play in its proper context, the Shakespearean canon.

277. Nicholls, Graham. *"Measure for Measure": Text and Performance.* London: Macmillan Education, 1986.

Consistent with the design of this student series, Nicholls's book is divided into two parts. The first deals with the themes of *Measure* using the tools of literary criticism, while the second discusses and compares interpretive choices made in performance, concentrating on John Barton's 1970 RSC production, the 1975 adaptation written and directed by Charles Marowitz at the Open Space Theatre, Barry Kyle's 1978 RSC production, and Desmond Davis's 1979 BBC TV production. These choices, selected as representative of recent performances, span a wide range of artistic intentions. In Davis's production, "the text was hardly touched, costumes and setting were traditional, characterization was straightforward" (54). At the opposite extreme, Marowitz's radical reshaping of the text ensures that "we know that this is **his** *Measure for Measure* and not Shakespeare's" (57).

I. Collections.

278. Bloom, Harold, ed. *William Shakespeare's "Measure for Measure."* Modern Critical Interpretations. New York: Chelsea House, 1987.

This collection reprints nos. 217, 236, 255, 256, 257, and 262. Bloom's brief introduction (1–6) is filled with opinions about the play and its characters ("Vienna in *Measure* is Isabella's vision.... The entire drama can be regarded as her version of the return of the repressed" [6]). Essays by M. C. Bradbrook on justice in *Measure* (7–21) and Harold C. Goddard on power (23–43) are also included. A brief bibliography completes the volume.

279. Wheeler, Richard P., ed. *Critical Essays on Shakespeare's "Measure for Measure."* Critical Essays on British Literature. New York: G. K. Hall, 1999.

This collection reprints nos. 208, 211, 213, 219, 226, and 228 among others. All essays are from works first published in the last two decades of the twentieth century, and the volume by design includes a variety of critical approaches from psychoanalytical analysis to cultural materialism. Wheeler's introduction (1-16) offers a succinct survey of the major critical treatments of *Measure* from the seventeenth century to the present. A selection by Katherine Eisaman Maus (197-216) discusses the relationship between characters' inward, subjective worlds and the external domain of society and its laws. Harry Berger, Jr. (217-28) writes about the relationships among Lucio, the Duke, and the Duke's alter-ego, the Friar.

J. Bibliographies; Concordances; Listings.

See nos. 200, 278.

INDEX I: AUTHORS AND EDITORS (SECTIONS II–V)

Index I includes the authors and editors of the books and articles collected in this bibliography. Authors, editors, directors, and actors whose work is discussed in the annotations are included in Index II. Citations are to item number.

Adams, Howard C., 71
Adelman, Janet, 72, 73, 139, 219, 279
Alexander, Peter, 48. *See also* Index II
Allen, David G., 184
Asp, Carolyn, 140
Astington, John H., 203

Barfoot, C. C., 66
Battenhouse, Roy, 204. *See also* Index II
Bawcutt, N. W., 199
Bayley, John, 74
Beale, Simon Russell, 107
Beauregard, David N., 126
Beckerman, Bernard, 43
Bednarz, James P., 54
Bennett, Josephine Waters, 141, 220. *See also* Index II
Bennett, Robert B., 205
Bentley, Eric, 270
Berger, Harry, Jr., 75, 279
Bergeron, David M., 127, 142
Bernhardt, W. W., 76
Bernthal, Craig A., 206
Beroud, Elizabeth, 108
Berry, Ralph, 109
Berthoff, Warner, 143
Bevington, David, 28, 43a, 184
Bloom, Harold, 278
Bly, Mary, 144

Boas, Frederick S., 29. *See also* Index II
Bowers, Fredson, 121, 122
Bradbrook, M. C., 278
Brecht, Bertolt, 270. *See also* Index II
Briggs, Julia, 145
Brockbank, Philip, 189
Brooks, Harold, 77
Brown, Carolyn E., 221
Bulman, J. C., 188
Burns, M. M., 78

Cacicedo, Albert, 222
Cairns, Edward A., 272
Calderwood, James L., 146, 147
Campbell, Oscar James, 79. *See also* Index II
Carey, John, 122
Carson, Neil, 185
Cartelli, Thomas, 148
Cary, Cecile Williamson, 198
Charnes, Linda, 80
Clarke, Larry R., 55
Cloud, Random (*aka* McLeod, Randall), 123
Cohen, Eileen Z., 149
Cole, Douglas, 56
Cole, Howard C., 128
Coles, Jane, 275
Colie, Rosalie L., 67
Cosman, Bard C., 129

Coursen, H. R., 188
Cox, John D., 206a
Crane, Mary Thomas, 223
Cunningham, Karen, 207

Danson, Lawrence, 68
Dash, Irene G., 186
Davenant, William, 271. See also Index II
Dawson, Anthony B., 224
Desmet, Christy, 137
Diehl, Huston, 225
DiGangi, Mario, 226, 279
Dodd, Mark Robert, 81
Dodd, William, 227
Dollimore, Jonathan, 82, 228, 279
Donaldson, E. Talbot, 57
Donaldson, Ian, 150
Dryden, John, 117. See also Index II
Dusinberre, Juliet, 83
Dutton, Richard, 42, 179, 207

Eagleton, Terence, 84, 229
Eccles, Mark, 200
Edens, Walter, 276
Ellis, David, 151
Empson, William, 85, 218
Engle, Lars, 230
Evans, Gareth Lloyd, 30

Fenwick, Henry, 265
Findlay, Alison, 152
Finney, Gail, 144
Fly, Richard D., 86
Foakes, R. A., 31, 110
Fraser, Russell, 118
Freund, Elizabeth, 58
Friedman, Michael D., 153, 187, 231
Frye, Northrop, 32. See also Index II

Garner, Shirley Nelson, 73
Gibbons, Brian, 201
Gibson, Rex, 275
Gildon, Charles, 272
Girard, René, 87

Glasser, Marvin, 59
Gless, Darryl J., 232
Goddard, Harold C., 278
Godshalk, W. L., 130
Goldberg, Jonathan, 208, 279
Grady, Hugh, 230
Greenblatt, Stephen, 209, 260. See also Index II
Greene, Gayle, 69, 88
Greenfield, Matthew A., 89
Greg, W. W., 49. See also Index II
Gross, Gerald J., 154
Gurr, Andrew, 233

Haley, David, 155
Halio, Jay L., 156, 197
Hall, Jonathan, 157, 234
Hamilton, A. C., 276
Hammersmith, James, 28
Hammond, Paul, 210
Harris, Sharon M., 90
Hartman, Geoffrey, 58, 87
Hawkins, Harriet, 235, 236. See also Index II
Hayne, Victoria, 211, 279
Hillebrand, Harold N., 44
Hillman, David, 70
Hodgdon, Barbara, 111, 158
Honigmann, E. A. J., 50, 51
Howard, Jean E., 42, 179, 207, 237
Hunt, Maurice, 138
Hunter, G. K., 119, 188
Huston, J. Dennis, 159
Hutchings, Geoffrey, 189
Hyland, Peter, 91

Ide, Richard S., 238
Innes, Sheila, 198a

Jackson, Russell, 107
James, Heather, 60
Jankowski, Theodora A., 239
Jardine, Lisa, 131
Jensen, Phebe, 52

military, 128, 153
Miller, Jonathan, 116
mock-heroic, 47
modernism, 55, 230
monasticism, 232. See also convent; Poor Clares
money, 62
Montaigne, Michel de, 230
—*Apology for Raymond Sebond*, 230
mooting, 207
morality, 228
morality play, see genre-morality play
Moshinsky, Elijah, 183, 197, 198
mother, 40, 72, 73, 152, 158, 166, 222
music, 199, 200, 202, 271, 272. See also song
mute characters, 202
myth, 32, 56, 89
—Christian, 204

nation state, 157, 164, 234
nationalism, 89
nature, 157
Nelligan, Kate, 265
Nietzsche, Friedrich, 70
Noble, Adrian, 265a
Nunn, Trevor, 189, 194, 197

Oberon (*Midsummer Night's Dream*), 174
opening scene, 156, 164, 168, 184, 196
order, 82, 91, 94, 101, 213, 246
Orlando (*As You Like It*), 40
outsider, 229

Painter, William, *Palace of Pleasure*, 118, 119, 120, 168, 199
paintings, see art
Pandarus (*TC*), 52, 76, 87, 101, 108
parable, see genre-parable
Paracelsus, Philippus Aureolus, 136, 176
pardon, 203, 206, 266
Paris (*TC*), 60
parody, 29, 68, 99, 127, 142

Parolles (*AW*), 31, 119, 124, 127, 130, 132, 133, 142, 151, 153, 154, 155, 156, 159, 161, 163, 167, 169, 174, 184, 186, 187, 190, 193
passion, 72. See also desire
patriarchy, patriarchal, 40, 41, 101, 140, 157, 174, 186, 188, 191, 192, 195, 198, 214, 239, 244, 255, 258, 260
Patroclus (*TC*), 99, 101, 107
patron, 50
patronage, 263
Payne, Iden, 111
Perdita (*Winter's Tale*), 165
performance at court, see court performance
Pericles (*Pericles*), 40
petrarchan, 144, 152
Phelps, Samuel, 193
Phillips, Robin, 264
Phoenix, see Middleton, Thomas
photographs and illustrations of productions, see illustrations
Pigott-Smith, Tim, 265
pilgrimage, 126, 174
Pisan, Christine de, 118
plague, 136
Plato, 137, 216
—*Hippias*, 83
playwrights, 37, 208, 214, 237
—characters as 37, 148, 225, 237, 248, 255
pleasure, in audience, 209, 226
Poets' War, see War of the Poets
politics, 35, 42, 61, 99, 176, 179, 181, 208, 210, 216, 224, 250
Pompey (*MM*), 31, 227, (Davenant, *Law Against Lovers*), 271
Poor Clares (monastic order), 232, 233, 258
Popham, Sir John, 213
power, 61, 64, 91, 183, 202, 206, 208, 214, 223, 224, 234, 235, 245, 255, 278
—feminine, 111, 139, 177, 194, 226

language, 28; (in *AW*), 39, 135, 137, 138, 144, 148, 158, 160, 161, 164, 165, 169, 172, 177, 184, 198a; (in *MM*), 217, 218, 221, 223, 226, 229, 230, 237, 241, 243, 253, 256, 264, 266; (in *TC*), 46, 62, 66, 67, 68, 69, 70, 71, 78, 80, 83, 85, 86, 93, 137. See also rhetoric
Lavache (Lavatch) (*AW*), 30, 151, 155, 158, 173, 189
law, 131, 206a, 207, 211, 212, 213, 215, 216, 228, 229, 233, 240, 256, 273
—marriage, 134, 222
Law Against Lovers, see Davanant, William
law courts, 216
Leavis, F. R., 256, 259. See also Index I
Leontes (*Winter's Tale*), 40
letter, 53, 138, 142, 175, 186, 202
lighting, in productions, 108
London, 205, 213
Lord E (*AW*), 163
love, 56, 67, 79, 87, 98, 100, 106, 144, 147, 149, 152, 177, 180, 201
Loves labours wonne, 119
Loyola, Saint Francis, 217
Lucio (*MM*), 31, 206a, 223, 227, 229, 231, 232, 233, 237, 238, 241, 246, 255, 274, 279
Lydgate, John, 39

Machiavelli, Niccolo, *Prince*, 214, 216
Mairet, Jean de, 238
Malvolio (*Twelfth Night*), 188
Margarelon (*TC*), 91
Mariana (*MM*), 33, 34, 204, 215, 221, 222, 226, 248, 264, 271
Marina (*Pericles*), 165
market, for drama, 42
marketplace, 250
Markham, Sir Griffin, 206
Marowitz, Charles, 267, 277. See also Index I

marriage, 31, 41, 120, 134, 135, 145, 149, 153, 154, 158, 170, 171, 176, 178, 181, 187, 211, 213, 215, 222, 226, 228, 229, 231, 242, 252, 258, 260, 261
marriage contracts, 135,199, 215, 229
marriage liturgy, 172
marriage proposal, see proposal, of marriage
Mars, 55, 127, 167
Marston, John, 31, 54, 79, 251
—*Antonio and Mellida*, 82
—*Antonio's Revenge*, 82
—*Malcontent*, 201, 235, 253
Marx, Karl, 157, 234
Mary (mother of Jesus), 206a
Mary Magdalene, 206a
masculinity, 139, 191, 219
masks, 108, 233
masochism, 35, 236
maternal, see body, maternal; mother
McGuire, Philip C., 266. See also Index I
Measure for Measure (act and scene)
—(2.1), 226
—(3.1), 39, 256, 258, 262, 266
—(5.1), 30, 203, 212, 214, 217, 219, 224, 238, 244, 245, 250, 264, 266, 267
medical debates, 136, 176
medical practice, 179
medicine, 128, 131, 136, 138, 176, 178. See also cure
—spiritual, 232
memory, 178, 194
Mendes, Sam, 107, 108
mercy, 38, 173, 206, 212, 215, 222, 259, 275
Meres, Francis, 119
metadramatic, see critical approaches, metadramatic
Middleton, Thomas, 251
—*Mad World My Masters*, 263
—*Phoenix*, 42, 201, 240, 253
miles gloriosus, see braggart soldier

Helen of Troy, 65, 124
Helena (*AW*), 29, 32, 34, 35, 40, 119, 120, 122, 123, 124, 127, 129, 130, 131, 132, 133, 134, 136, 137, 139, 140, 143, 144, 146, 147, 148, 149, 152, 154, 155, 156, 157, 159, 160, 161, 162, 163, 164, 166, 167, 168, 170, 173, 174, 175, 177, 178, 179, 180, 182, 184, 186, 187, 188, 191, 192, 193, 194, 195, 196, 197, 198, 198a
Helena (*Midsummer Night's Dream*), 174
Heminge (also Heminges), John, 49
Henryson, Robert, *Testament of Cressid*, 47
Henslowe, Philip, 42
hermit, 212
Herring, Francis, 176
Heywood, Thomas
—*If You Know Me You Know Nobody*, 42
—*Iron Age*, 44, 89
Hitler, Adolf, 270
Homer, *Iliad*, 58, 65
honor, 38, 77, 96, 106, 147, 155, 157, 167, 181
Hooker, Richard, 216
humanism, 82, 131, 205, 217
Hytner, Nicholas, 201

idealism, idealist, 56, 77, 97, 98, 205, 220
illustrations, 155, 190, 251
—of productions, 36, 43, 43b, 120, 195, 198a, 199, 201, 265, 275
imagery, 38, 63, 66, 115, 129
incest, 258
individual, individualism, 84, 216, 229
Inns of Court, 45, 52, 53, 207
intertextuality, 43b, 57, 58, 65, 80, 96
Isabel (Davenant, *Law Against Lovers*), 271
Isabella (*MM*), 29, 31, 33, 34, 35, 38, 39, 40, 41, 137, 149, 165, 199, 205, 212, 213, 214, 215, 217, 219, 220, 221, 223, 225, 226, 231, 232, 233, 236, 238, 239, 242, 243, 244, 245, 247, 248, 250, 251, 252, 256, 258, 261, 264, 265, 266, 267, 269, 276, 278
Isbel (*AW*), 189

James I, 35, 41, 62, 176, 199, 201, 203, 206, 208, 210, 213, 214, 225, 248, 249, 250, 257, 259, 260
—*Basilicon Doron*, 201, 220, 232, 249, 257, 259
Jamieson, Michael, 36
Jesus, 129, 244, 265a
—*Sermon on the Mount*, 232
Joan of Arc (*1 Henry VI*), 184
Johnson, Samuel, 150
Jonson, Ben, 31, 54, 79
—*Everyman in his Humour*, 42
—*Everyman out of his Humour*, 42
—*Poetaster*, 54
—*Sejanus*, 201
Joseph (step-father of Jesus), 206a
Judah (*Genesis*), 172
Juliet (Julietta) (*MM*), 135, 209, 215, 219, 226, 236, 264, (Davenant, *Law Against Lovers*), 271
justice, 206, 210, 212, 216, 232, 238, 243, 257, 259, 275, 278

Kemble, John Philip, 112, 190, 192, 193. *See also* Index I
King (*AW*), 32, 40, 126, 127, 129, 136, 137, 139, 140, 142, 148, 153, 155, 157, 159, 163, 168, 170, 171, 175, 178, 182, 184, 187, 188, 194, 197, 198
Knight, G. Wilson, 205, 256. *See also* Index I
Knights, L. C., 167, 247
Kyle, Barry, 111, 194, 264, 267, 277

Lacan, Jacques, 101, 140, 157, 175, 234
Lafew (*AW*), 31, 121, 154, 163, 164

folk tales, 32, 33, 179
folkways, 135
fool, 34, 151, 154, 169, 271
forgetting, 178
forgiveness, 39, 220
fornication, 201, 205, 211, 213, 245
Foucault, Michel, 161, 250
foul papers, 50, 53, 119, 120, 121, 199
French Lords (*AW*), 121, 122, 124, 185
Freud, Sigmund, 140, 157, 234
friar (*MM*), 41, 203, 211, 233, 251, 258, 279
friendship, 140
Frye, Northrop, 38, 182. See also Index I

Galen, 136, 176
Garrick, David, 190, 192
gaze, 111, 191
gender, 35, 64, 100, 111, 183, 191, 198a, 245. See also critical approaches–feminism and gender studies
generational conflict and relationships, 156, 159, 164, 166, 168, 170, 173, 181, 182, 183, 195
genre, 42, 43a, 43b, 47, 50, 51, 52, 50, 77, 78, 79, 120, 195, 227, 237, 254, 260, 264, 266, 276
—comedy, 127, 160, 169, 171, 182, 192, 210, 220, 235, 255, 259, 262. See also genre, romantic comedy
—epithalamion, 172
—farce, 192
—festive comedy, see genre, romantic comedy
—heroic drama, 67, 76
—history play, 81
—melodrama, 192, 193
—morality play, 130, 217, 238
—mystery play, 206a
—novella, 212
—parable, 204, 244
—romance, 31, 32, 39, 40, 67, 119, 136, 141, 162, 165, 166, 181, 182, 192, 205
—Roman new comedy, 133
—romantic comedy, 31, 32, 40, 127, 140, 144, 165, 182
—sermon, 172
—sonnets, 40
—tragedy, 40, 50, 51, 52, 68, 76, 82, 92, 104, 116, 117, 127, 144, 169, 227, 235, 276
—tragicomedy, 201, 227, 235, 238, 242, 246a, 256, 261, 266
Gentleman, Francis, 112
Geoffrey of Monmouth, 60
Gildon, Charles, 246a, 272. See also Index I
Giles, David, 264
Gill, Peter, 267
Giraldi, Giambattista Cinzio (Cinthio), *Hecatomithi*, 200, 201, 202, 246a
Goneril (*King Lear*), 123
grace, 126, 132, 225, 242
Greeks, 39, 55, 60, 74, 78, 94, 96, 98, 99, 108, 116
Greenblatt, Stephen, 240. See also Index I
green sickness, 179
Greg, W. W., 53. See also Index I
Grey, Lord, 206
Guthrie, Tyrone, 30, 109, 115, 185, 197

Hack, Keith, 264, 267
Hall, John, 136
Hall, Peter, 111
Hampton Court
—conference at, 225
—productions at, 203, 220
Hands, Terry, 111
Hawkins, Harriet, 232. See also Index I
healer, 131, 179
healing, 127, 142, 146. See also cure
Hector (*TC*), 30, 56, 61, 77, 78, 89, 95, 96, 117
Helen (*TC*), 56, 60, 61, 62, 65, 78, 83

critical surveys, 36, 38, 43, 86, 90, 146, 183, 192, 206, 251, 254, 259, 279
cuckold, cuckoldry, 89, 181
cure, 40, 126, 136, 137, 140, 142, 147, 156, 158, 163, 171, 175, 194, 197. *See also* healing

dark comedy, *see* genre, tragicomedy
Davenant, William. *See also* Index I
—*Law Against Lovers*, 199, 201, 246a, 251, 272
Davies, Howard, 111, 115
Davis, Desmond, 111, 264, 265, 277
death, 32, 68, 150, 156, 181, 217, 242
debasement (of coins), 62
Decameron, *see* Boccaccio, Giovanni
decapitation, 212
decrepitude, 166
degree, Ulysses' speech on, *see* *Troilus and Cressida*, 1.3
Dekker, Thomas
—*Blurt Master Constable*, 144
—*Shoemaker's Holiday*, 42
Deleuze, Gilles, 157, 234
desire, 87, 105, 139, 140, 144, 145, 166, 175, 178, 191, 213, 219, 229, 238, 252, 260, 261
despair, 217
devil, 212
De Witt, Johannes, 28
Diana (*AW*), 34, 124, 127, 133, 135, 142, 144, 167, 175, 178, 191
Diana (goddess), 124, 127
Diomedes (*TC*), 71, 77, 92, 104, 111, 112b
directors' interpretations, 30, 36, 43, 108, 112a, 114, 116, 265
disease, 83, 101, 105, 108, 156, 164
disguise, 149, 203, 204, 211, 241, 251
disguised ruler, disguised-ruler play, 201, 202, 240, 251, 253, 260
double, 124, 142, 158
double plot, 85, 102
Dowden, Edward, 38
dramatic competition, 42

dramatis personae, 123
dramaturg, 184
Dryden, John, *Truth Found Too Late*, 76, 89, 117. *See also* Index I
Duke (*MM*), *see* Vincentio

eavesdropping, 104, 112b
Edgerton, Thomas, 216
effeminacy, 64
Elbow, Mistress (*MM*), 226
Elizabeth I, 35, 61, 62, 127, 176, 213, 214, 216, 260
Elliot, Michael, 265a
Elyot, Thomas, *Image of Governaunce*, 201
empirics, 136, 176, 179
ending, 29, 50, 134, 138, 140, 150, 162, 177, 178, 180, 199, 220, 224, 225, 230, 234, 238, 247, 251, 256, 261. *See also* closure
epilogue, 52, 117, 148
epistemology, 59, 176
Erasmus, Desiderius, 205
—*Colloquies*, 120, 172, 232
Essex, second earl of, 43b, 50, 51, 60, 61, 79
exchange, 62, 105, 201

Fair Maid of Bristow, 203
fairy tales, 38, 147
—*Beauty and the Beast*, 191
—*Cinderella*, 191, 197
father, 166, 219, 244, 258, 260
fatherhood, 153, 166
felix culpa, 242
Fenwick, Henry, 265
festive comedy, *see* genre, romantic comedy
film and television versions, 188, 198, 265. *See also* BBC
fistula, 129, 136, 164, 179
folio text (*AW*), 118, 119, 120, 121, 125, 164, 185; (*MM*), 199, 200, 201, 202, 246a, 271, 272; (*TC*), 43a, 43b, 44, 46, 47, 48, 49, 50, 53

253, 254, 256, 267, 269, 276; (in *TC*), 47, 57, 58, 59, 74, 76, 80, 86, 95, 107, 108, 115
Charles V of France, 129
chastity, 35, 124, 165, 167, 252, 258, 276
Chaucer, Geoffrey, *Troilus and Criseyde*, 57, 58, 97
Chevalereux Comte d'Artois, 128
China, theater in, 199
chivalry, 29, 61, 63
Christ, *see* Jesus
christianity, christian doctrine, 138, 204, 216, 244, 254, 256, 258. *See also* religion
Church of England, 126
Cicero, 137, 243
Cinthio, *see* Giraldi, Giambattista Cinzio
city, 252. *See also* London
class struggle, 55
Claudio (*MM*), 33, 40, 187, 206, 209, 215, 231, 232, 236, 237, 248, 255, 256, 264, 266, (Davenant, *Law Against Lovers*), 271
closure, 34, 38, 50, 79, 148, 154, 161, 207, 245. *See also* ending
Clown (*AW*), 124, 175, 189. *See also* fool
Cobham, Lord, 206
cognitive theory, 223
Coke, Sir Edward, 213
comedy, *see* genre, comedy
commerce, 62, 63, 66, 88
commercialism, 263
commodification, 64, 65, 78, 88, 100, 101, 152
community, 89, 98, 145, 152, 216, 263
—of women, 174
complementarity, 102
compositors, 121, 122
Condell, Henry, 49
convent, 232, 261, 262
conversion, 263
costumes, 35, 108, 116, 233, 251, 277

Cotta, John, 176
Council of Trent, 215
Count of Roussillon (*AW*–Bertram's dead father), 138, 153, 178
Countess of Roussillon (*AW*–Bertram's mother), 40, 121, 123, 138, 139, 157, 163, 164, 168, 184, 186, 189
court, 61, 128, 155, 210
court, law, *see* law court
court factions, 53, 61
court performance, 203, 220
court wards, 41, 164
courtier, 155
courtly love, 63
Crane, Ralph, 201
Cressida (*TC*), 29, 34, 35, 47, 57, 58, 60, 61, 62, 65, 71, 72, 73, 78, 82, 83, 85, 88, 89, 90, 92, 94, 95, 97, 98, 100, 101, 104, 106, 111, 112a, 113, 115, 116, 165
Criseyde (Chaucer, *Troilus and Criseyde*), 57
critical approaches, 279
—cultural materialist and new historicist, 61, 82, 208, 209, 223, 224, 228, 240, 245, 249, 260, 263, 279
—feminist and gender studies, 35, 64, 88, 90, 100, 111, 137, 139, 152, 186, 187, 191, 194, 219, 226, 239, 245
—formalist, 86, 238
—genre, 32
—Marxist, 63, 157
—metadramatic, 37, 148, 225, 237, 263
—performance, 35, 95, 107, 108, 111, 112a, 112b, 113, 115, 116, 153, 183, 184, 185, 186, 187, 188, 189, 191, 194, 195, 196, 197, 198, 224, 227, 231, 264, 265, 265a, 266, 267, 268, 269, 277
—psychoanalytical, 35, 40, 72, 80, 101, 102, 139, 140, 157, 191, 212, 219, 221, 236, 279
—structuralist, 143
critical reception, 36

audience, audience response, 29, 33, 42, 43b, 59, 66, 67, 73, 74, 85, 95, 96, 103, 104, 112, 112b, 113, 132, 141, 148, 149, 152, 157, 183, 201, 207, 209, 214, 227, 234, 240, 247, 254, 273, 276
authority, 38, 91, 109, 202, 222, 223, 227, 230
autonomy, 202, 213, 255

BBC Shakespeare productions, 116, 183, 188, 194, 197, 198, 264, 265, 267, 277
Bacon, Francis, *Advancement of Learning*, 176
Bakhtin, Mikhail, 91, 157, 234, 250
Barber, C. L., 40, 182
Barnardine (*MM*), 206, 212, 214, 216, 237, 248, 255, 256, 264, 267
Barton, John, 30, 36, 111, 265a, 267, 269, 277
Bassanio (*Merchant of Venice*), 40
bastard, bastardy, 89, 91, 258
Battenhouse, Roy, 205, 259. See also Index I
Beatrice (Davenant, *Law Against Lovers*), 271
beauty, 71, 83
bed-trick, 35, 41, 139, 141, 142, 144, 145, 146, 149, 158, 165, (biblical) 172, 175, 184, 191, 195, 202, 225, 248, 251
Benedick (Davenant, *Law Against Lovers*), 271
Bennett, Josephine, 265. See also Index I
Benthall, Michael, 197
Bertram (*AW*), 28, 29, 34, 38, 40, 41, 119, 120, 121, 124, 127, 130, 131, 132, 133, 134, 135, 138, 139, 140, 142, 144, 145, 146, 147, 148, 149, 151, 152, 153, 154, 155, 156, 157, 159, 160, 161, 162, 164, 166, 167, 168, 170, 173, 175, 178, 179, 180, 182, 186, 187, 190, 191, 194, 195, 196, 197, 198

betrothal, 211
Biblical references, 155, 172
bildungsroman, 76, 124
blocking, theatrical, 108, 112b, 113, 184, 227
Blurt Master Constable, see Dekker, Thomas
Boas, F. S., 33. See also Index I
Boccaccio, Giovanni, *Decameron*, 118, 119, 120, 128, 129, 158, 168, 183, 201
body, 101, 105, 250
—maternal, 139, 152, 219
—politicization of, 208
bonding, male, 187
boys' theater companies, see theaters and theater companies, early modern–boys'
braggart soldier (*miles gloriosus*), 133
Brecht, Bertolt, 35. See also Index I
Brook, Peter, 268, 269
—*Empty Space*, 268
Bucer, Martin, 216
buffo, 94
Burge, Stuart, 267

Calchas (*TC*), 89, (Dryden, *Troilus*), 117
Calvin, John, 217, 225
calvinism, 132, 217, 225
Cambridge, theater performances at, 50
Campbell, Oscar James, 103. See also Index I
capitalism, 63
carnival, carnivalesque, 91, 234
catholicism, see Roman Catholicism; religion
Catullus, 172
Chapman, George
—*Homer*, 60
—*Humorous Day's Mirth*, 42
character, characterization, 30, 39, 42, 44; (in *AW*), 120, 141, 143, 147, 168; (in *MM*), 199, 218, 251, 252,

INDEX II: SUBJECTS
(SECTIONS II–V)

The following indexes the annotations in sections II–V. Titles of texts (including Shakespeare's except for *TC*, *AW*, and *MM*) are listed under the author's name. *TC*, *AW*, and *MM* are listed in the index when specific acts and scenes are discussed in the annotations; act and scene numbers are listed sequentially under the title of each play. Characters are listed individually. Citations are to item number.

Accolti, Bernardo, *Virginia*, 128
Achilles (*TC*), 34, 56, 61, 64, 77, 79, 89, 107
adultery, 206a, 211
Ahab (*Book of Kings, Old Testament*), 155
AIDS, 105
Ajax (*TC*), 34, 54, 79, 87
alchemy, 129, 155
Alexander, Peter, 45. See also Index I
allegory, 232, 244, 259
All's Well that Ends Well (act and scene)
—(1.1), 125, 156, 164, 184, 196
—(1.2), 188
—(1.3), 122
—(2.1), 129, 184, 185
—(2.3), 122, 184, 187, 194
—(2.5), 187
—(3.5), 185
—(3.7), 184
—(4.1), 169, 185, 188
—(4.3), 122, 151, 153, 161, 175, 188, 191
—(5), 140, 154
—(5.1), 175
—(5.3), 150, 153, 156, 160, 162, 170, 175, 184, 188, 191, 197

ambiguity, 34, 57, 132, 134, 215, 218, 254, 256
ambivalence, 124, 131, 137
Andromache (Dryden, John, *Truth Found Too Late*), 117
Angelo (*MM*), 31, 33, 34, 35, 38, 40, 41, 137, 145, 206, 212, 213, 214, 215, 216, 217, 219, 220, 221, 222, 223, 225, 231, 232, 234, 236, 237, 238, 239, 242, 244, 245, 247, 248, 250, 251, 252, 264, 265, 265a, 267, (Davenant, *Law Against Lovers*) 271
Antenor (*TC*), 70
anti-heroic, 64
anxiety, 105, 157, 209, 234, 240
appetite, 70, 109
Arderne, John, 129
Ariosto, Lodovico, 60
aristocracy, 55
Aristotle, 32, 216, 243
—*Ethics*, 45
Armin, Robert, 155
art, painting, 59, 127, 198
Artaud, Antonin, 273
Astyanax (Dryden, *Truth Found Too Late*), 117
atonement, 204

Rossiter, A. P., 256
Rutter, Carol, 194

Salmon, Vivian, 46
Samuelson, David A., 113
Schleiner, Louise, 257
Scott, Margaret, 215
Scott, Michael, 267
Shallcross, Alan, 265
Shapiro, Michael, 170
Shattuck, Charles H., 190
Shell, Marc, 258
Shuger, Debra Kuller, 216
Shurgot, Michael, 112b
Silverman, J. M., 171
Simonds, Peggy Muñoz, 172
Sinfield, Alan, 228
Slavitt, David R., 274
Slights, Camille, 103
Smallwood, R. L., 173
Smallwood, Robert, 107
Snyder, Susan, 120, 124, 174, 175
Solomon, Julie Robin, 176
Southall, Raymond, 63
Spear, Gary, 64
Spinrad, Phoebe S., 217
Sprengnether, Madelon, 73
Sprigg, Douglas C., 113
Stallybrass, Peter, 123
Stamm, Rudolph, 114
Stanton, Kay, 177
Stein, Arnold, 104
Stensgaard, Richard K., 136
Stevenson, David Lloyd, 259
Storey, Graham, 256
Styan, J. L., 195, 196. See also Index II
Sullivan, Garrett A., Jr., 178

Suzuki, Mihoko, 65

Taborski, Boleslaw, 94
Taylor, Gary, 46, 53, 125
Tennenhouse, Leonard, 260
Thomas, Vivian, 38
Thompson, Marvin, 110
Thompson, Ruth, 110
Thomson, Peter, 193
Tillyard, E. M. W., 39. See also Index II
Traister, Barbara Howard, 179
Traub, Valerie, 105
Turner, Robert Kean, 28
Tylee, Claire M., 115

Walker, Alice, 47. See also Index II
Waller, Gary, 140
Warren, Roger, 180, 197
Watson, Robert N., 261
Weil, Herbert, Jr., 262, 268, 278
Wells, Stanley, 36, 46
Welsh, Alexander, 181
Wheeler, Richard P., 40, 182, 279
White, Robert A., 184
Willard, Helen D., 269
Williams, Michele, 161
Williamson, Jane, 269
Williamson, Marilyn L., 41
Willis, Susan, 116, 198
Willson, Robert F., Jr., 196

Yachnin, Paul, 42, 263
Yoder, R. A., 106
Young, C. B., 47

Zitner, Sheldon P., 183

INDEX I: AUTHORS AND EDITORS

Kahane, Claire, 73
Kamps, Ivo, 240
Kaplan, M. Lindsay, 241
Kastan, David Scott, 28, 123, 160
Kaufmann, A. J., 92
Kemble, John Philip, 190. *See also* Index II
Kendall, Gillian Murray, 250
Kettle, Arnold, 63
Kimbrough, Robert, 93
Kirsch, Arthur, 242
Kliman, Bernice W., 243
Knight, G. Wilson, 244. *See also* Index II
Knoppers, Laura Lungers, 245
Kott, Jan, 94

Labranche, Linda, 95
Lamb, Mary Ellen, 246
Laroque, François, 161
Lascelles, Mary, 246a
Lawrence, William Witherle, 33
Leavis, F. R., 247. *See also* Index II
Leggatt, Alexander, 162, 248
Lenz, Carolyn, 88
Leonard, Nancy S., 34
Lever, J. W., 202
Levin, Carole, 71
Levin, Richard, 249
Levin, Richard A., 163, 164
Lewis, Cynthia, 132
Limouze, Henry S., 198
Little, Arthur L., Jr., 250
Lupton, Julia Reinhard, 212
Lynch, Stephen J., 96, 97, 98

Mack, Peter, 99
Mahon, John W., 77, 166, 253
Mallin, Eric S., 61
Maquin, Jean-Marie, 161
Marcus, Leah S., 213, 279
Marowitz, Charles, 273. *See also* Index II
Maus, Katherine Eisaman, 279
McCandless, David, 35, 165, 191

McGann, Jerome J., 50
McGuire, Paul C., 113
McGuire, Philip C., 264. *See also* Index II
McLeod, Randall, *see* Cloud, Random
Mead, Stephen X., 62
Merrix, Robert P., 177
Messina, Cedric, 265
Miles, Rosalind, 251
Miola, Robert S., 133
Moore, Don D., 265a
Morgan, Appleton, 271
Muir, Kenneth, 36, 197
Mukherji, Subha, 134
Mullaney, Steven, 214

Neely, Carol, 88
Nevo, Ruth, 166
Newlin, Jeanne T., 112
Nicholls, Graham, 277
Norbrook, David, 99
Novy, Marianne L., 100

O'Rourke, James, 101

Palmer, D. J., 197
Palmer, Kenneth, 45
Papp, Joseph, 28, 43, 112a
Parker, Patricia, 58, 87
Parker, R. B., 167
Paster, Gail Kern, 252
Pendleton, Thomas A., 77, 166, 253
Powers, Alan W., 135
Price, John Edward, 168
Price, Jonathan R., 254
Price, Joseph G., 112, 192, 269

Rabkin, Norman, 102
Ranson, Nicholas, 177
Richard, Jeremy, 169
Richards, Kenneth, 193
Riefer, Marcia, 255
Righter, Anne, 37
Robertson, Karen, 71
Rocklin, Edward L., 266

INDEX II: SUBJECTS

—masculine, 139, 219, 222, 226, 239
—monarchical, 41, 214, 227, 240, 250, 260
prayer, 126, 245
pregnancy, 133, 186, 211, 219
—male, 223
printing history, 43b, 44, 45, 47, 48, 49, 51, 53, 121, 200, 201
prison, 203, 217, 252
problem play, definition of, 29, 33, 35, 38, 39, 42, 51, 119, 160, 169, 199, 212, 247, 251, 259
procreation, 83, 146, 147, 153, 157, 179, 181, 222, 258, 261
production illustrations, photographs, *see* illustrations
prologue, 54, 75
promptbook, 53, 112, 119, 185, 186, 190, 193, 199, 268
proposal, of marriage, 205, 221, 231, 232, 238, 242, 245, 266, 268, 269. *See also* marriage contract
Prospero (*Tempest*), 237
prostitute, 47, 228, 245, 270
punishment, 31, 74, 241, 250
Purcell, Henry, *Dido and Aeneas*, 272
Puritans, English, 201, 205, 211, 216, 225. *See also* religion

quarto text, 43, 43a, 43b, 44, 45, 46, 47, 48, 49, 50, 51, 53, 272

Rabelais, François, *Tiers Livre*, 181
Raleigh, Sir Walter, 206
realism, 33, 38, 39, 144, 146, 158, 161, 162, 165, 192, 196, 197
reason, 84, 137, 210
redemption, 170
Reformation, 132; reformation, 225
religion, 132, 172, 212, 217, 230, 236, 242. *See also* Christianity; Puritanism; Roman Catholicism
repentance, 209, 217, 220
reported scenes, 114, 135, 158, 175
representation, 208, 211, 216, 225

reversal, 32
revision, by Shakespeare, 122, 199, 202
rhetoric, 58, 67, 69, 70, 75, 93, 99, 104, 106, 112, 137, 168, 243
riddles, 138, 158
ring, 133, 134, 147, 161, 178
Roman Catholicism, 126, 132, 213, 215, 225. *See also* religion
Roman new comedy, *see* genre, Roman new comedy
romance, *see* genre, romance
romantic comedy, *see* genre, romantic comedy
Rome, 60
Royal College of Physicians of London, 136
Royal Shakespeare Company, *see* theaters and theater companies (twentieth century), Royal Shakespeare
Rudall, Nick, 184

sadism, 35, 236
saints' lives, 212
satire, 29, 30, 31, 54, 79, 89, 103, 109, 230, 246, 251
scapegoat, 40, 65, 163
scene changes, 190
scepticism, 230
Scrutiny, 247
self-fashioning, 71, 152
sets, *see* stage sets
sexuality, 35, 40, 41, 64, 73, 100, 101, 139, 146, 147, 153, 158, 163, 165, 167, 172, 177, 179, 181, 183, 199, 206a, 214, 219, 221, 222, 226, 228, 239, 275
Shakespeare, William, 220, 254
—*As You Like It*, 40
—*Cymbeline*, 33
—*Hamlet*, 29, 39, 42, 143
—*Henry V*, 75
—*1 Henry VI*, 184
—*Julius Caesar*, 121
—*King Lear*, 123
—*Merchant of Venice*, 40, 131

—*Midsummer Night's Dream*, 174, 263
—*Much Ado About Nothing*, 187, 271
—*Pericles*, 40, 165
—*Richard III*, 125
—*Romeo and Juliet*, 100, 112a, 178
—*Sonnets*, 120, 153, 180
—*Tempest*, 237
—*Twelfth Night*, 188
—*Venus and Adonis*, 146
—*Winter's Tale*, 40, 165
shame, shaming, 167, 214, 221, 223, 245, 258
Shaw, Glen Byam, 111
Shoemaker's Holiday, see Dekker, Thomas
sickness, 161
silence, silencing, 68, 70, 137, 191, 196, 222, 241, 245, 264, 266
slander, 223, 231, 238, 241
social reform, 205
social responsibility, 84
social status, 55, 176, 178, 183
soliloquies, 73, 186
song, 199, 271. See also music
sonnets, see genre–sonnets
sources, 28, 29; (of *AW*), 118, 119, 120, 124, 127, 128, 129, 133, 145, 155, 158, 168, 172, 183; (of *MM*), 200, 201, 202, 203, 204, 206a, 207, 210, 212, 214, 217, 238, 243, 246a, 251, 253; (of *TC*), 38, 39, 43a, 43b, 44, 45, 47, 56, 57, 58, 60, 65, 93
sovereignty, 206a
speech act theory, 138
speech prefixes, 121, 122, 123, 124, 185
spelling and punctuation, Shakespeare's, 46
Spenser, Edmund, *Fairie Queene*, 65
spousals, see marriage contracts
Sprigg, Douglas C., 112b. See also Index I
stage directions, 46, 114, 122, 185, 194, 199, 273
stage history, 28, 30, 36; (of *AW*), 118, 120, 153, 183, 186, 190, 192, 193, 194, 195, 197; (of *MM*), 199, 200, 201, 231, 251, 264, 265a, 266, 267, 269, 277; (of *TC*), 43, 44, 47, 50, 109, 111, 112b, 115
stage sets, 267, 268, 277
staging, 110, 111, 187, 198a, 267
stereotype, 65, 95, 149
structure, dramatic, 39, 47, 85, 86, 93, 102, 103, 142, 147, 168, 171, 173, 184, 251, 255, 259, 261
Styan, J. L., 113. See also Index I
subjectivity, 65, 140, 178, 191
substitute, substitution, 34, 41, 158, 175, 202, 212, 225, 229, 241, 248, 252, 260, 265
subversion, subversive, 80, 82, 91, 172, 210, 224
syphilis, 105

Tamar (*Genesis*), 172
Tate, Nahum, 272
Taylor, Gary, 50, 52. See also Index I
television versions, see film and television versions
textual issues, see subsections III.B; IV.B; V.B
textual variants, 125
theater, as represented in plays, 37, 60, 246, 252. See also critical approaches, metadramatic
theaters and theater companies (pre-twentieth century)
—boys', 42
—Covent Garden, 190
—Globe, 52, 112b
—Henslowe's, 42
—King's Men, 51, 110
—Sadler's Wells, 193
—Swan, 28
—Theater, 112b
—Theatre Royal, 266
theaters and theater companies (twentieth century)
—Court (Chicago), 184
—Delacorte (New York City), 43, 112a

INDEX II: SUBJECTS 139

—Edinburgh Festival, 267
—Old Vic (London) 36, 109, 115, 197, 265a
—Open Space (London), 267, 277
—Riverside Studios (London), 267
—Royal Shakespeare (Stratford and London), 36, 38, 107, 108, 111, 115, 189, 194, 264, 265a, 267, 268, 269, 277
—Shakespeare Festival (Stratford, Ont.), 264, 269
—Shakespeare Memorial Theater (Stratford, UK), 111
theology, 126, 132, 204, 216, 257
Thersites (*TC*), 30, 54, 74, 75, 76, 89, 91, 101, 107, 108, 109
Tillyard, E. M. W., *Elizabethan World Picture*, 99. See also Index I
time, 39, 45, 59, 74, 82, 102, 114, 198, 201, 202
title page, 48, 51
topical allusions, 50, 51, 54, 55, 61, 62, 63, 79, 128, 129, 136, 199, 201, 202, 206, 210, 213, 216, 217, 220, 225, 227, 232, 248, 249, 250, 257, 259, 260
tragedy, see genre, tragedy
tragicomedy, see genre, tragicomedy
treason, 206
trickster, trickery, 131, 234
Troilus (*TC*), 29, 34, 39, 50, 52, 56, 57, 60, 64, 65, 71, 72, 73, 76, 77, 82, 88, 90, 92, 97, 100, 101, 106, 112a, 112b, 116
Troilus and Cressida (act and scene)
—(1.2), 111, 114
—(1.3—Ulysses' speech on degree), 44, 45, 75, 99, 109
—(4.5), 115
—(5.2), 104, 111, 112a, 113
—(5.5), 91
Trojan War, 29, 39, 74
Trojans, 39, 55, 74, 96, 98, 108, 116
Troy legend, 29, 39, 56, 58, 60, 63, 65, 89, 97, 117

Ulysses (*TC*), 39, 44, 45, 87, 89, 91, 99. See also *Troilus and Cressida*, 1.3

value, 43b, 62, 66, 69, 82, 84, 88, 92, 96, 102
Venus, 55, 124, 127, 167
Veronese, Paolo, 167
vice, 236, 238
Vincentio (*MM*), 33, 34, 37, 38, 40, 41, 199, 201, 202, 204, 205, 206a, 207, 208, 209, 213, 214, 215, 216, 217, 220, 221, 222, 223, 227, 229, 230, 231, 232, 233, 234, 235, 237, 238, 239, 240, 241, 242, 243, 244, 246, 247, 248, 250, 251, 252, 253, 255, 256, 257, 261, 264, 265a, 266, 267, 268, 269, 276, 279
Violetta (Dekker, *Blurt Master Constable*), 144
virgin, virginity, 124, 139, 153, 158, 167, 212, 226, 239
virtue, 38, 143, 157, 177, 202, 223, 236, 238
visual arts, 59, 167, 198, 201, 251. See also illustrations

Walker, Alice, 53. See also Index I
war, 56, 63, 65, 67, 78, 79, 83, 85, 87, 106, 153, 156, 167, 170, 177. See also Trojan War
War of the Poets, 54
wardship, see court ward
wealth, see money
Whetstone, George, 200, 201, 202, 204, 238
—*Heptameron*, 200
—*Mirrour for Magistrates of Cyties*, 201
—*Promos and Cassandra*, 200, 202, 204, 238, 246a
whore, 90, 98, 226
Widow (*AW*), 184
widow, 226
wound, 129